Angels *that* Gather

EMPOWERMENT FOR END-OF-THE-AGE HARVEST

PAUL KEITH DAVIS

DOVE COMPANY PUBLISHING
ORANGE BEACH, ALABAMA

Angels that Gather: Empowerment for End-of-the-Age-Harvest
Copyright © 2007 by Paul Keith Davis

To contact the author, please write:
WhiteDove Ministries, P.O. Box 2153, Foley, AL 36535

ISBN: 978-0-9794802-0-1

Creative Director: Shanee Clark
Editors: Dorian Kreindler, Mary Ballotte
Editorial Assistant: Bridgett Clark
Designed by Dustin Bocks
Cover by Dustin Bocks

Unless otherwise identified, all Scripture quotations in this publication are taken from the *New American Standard Bible* (NASB), © The Lockman Foundation 1960, 1962, 1963, 1968, 1971, 1972, 1973, 1975, 1977, and are used with permission.

Scripture quotations marked NKJV are taken from the New King James Version©. Copyright © 1982 by Thomas Nelson, Inc. Used by permission. All rights reserved.

Printed in the United States of America.

FOR MORE INFORMATION ON PAUL KEITH DAVIS'
BOOKS AND OTHER MATERIALS
CALL (251) 943–9669 OR VISIT
WWW.WHITEDOVEMINISTRIES.ORG

Contents

Introduction

The Bible characterizes our latter-day generation as one filled with spiritual activity. The veil separating the natural and spiritual realms has never before been as thin as at present. Our primary focus is on the Lord Jesus Christ rather than angels or created beings. Even so, as we mature and walk more intimately with Him, a heightened spiritual sensitivity will result and our eyes will be opened to perceive more of God's spiritual arena.

WIND AND FIRE

The writer of the book of Hebrews portrays both cooperation between the natural and supernatural realms and an exponential acceleration with a dynamic word picture. Of the angels He says:

> "WHO MAKES HIS ANGELS WINDS,
> AND HIS MINISTERS A FLAME OF FIRE."
> —Hebrews 1:7

In the natural, wind accelerates fire and causes it to spread rapidly. God's ministers are to likewise become such spiritual flames of fire, fueled by the high-velocity heavenly currents known as angels. Recognizing the fruit of this dimension is fundamental to apprehending it. End-time prophetic promises are not merely words on a page but must become experiential. They must become a living panorama beating in the heart of every believer.

The New Testament has meticulously recorded the supernatural activity of God's Spirit and His angelic host in the early Church. It is imperative we understand that their day was the time of sowing Kingdom seeds, while we are living in the harvesting generation. The time of reaping always multiplies what has been sown.

Paul admonished his spiritual son, Timothy, concerning the challenges of their generation and compared them to a future day that would be even worse. They clearly encountered hardships and difficulties launching the Good News of God's Kingdom, but he went on to outline the latter-days as even more troublesome. He said:

> But realize this, in the last days difficult times will come. For men will be lovers of self, lovers of money, boastful, arrogant, revilers, disobedient to parents, ungrateful, unholy, unloving, irreconcilable, malicious gossips, without self-control, brutal, haters of good, treacherous, reckless, conceited, lovers of pleasure rather than lovers of God, holding to a form of godliness, although they have denied its power...
> —2 Timothy 3:1–5

If the first-century Church was marked by intervention from God's Spirit and His angelic host to accomplish its divine mandates, how much more do we require that same support to meet the manifold demands of our generation? Spiritual influences that proved difficult in the lives of the early apostles have grown, like cultivated trees, into established forces; likewise the "sons of the Kingdom" must mature and rise to wield Kingdom power and authority also!

Without utilizing the powerful legacy clearly introduced by the early Pentecostal age, we simply cannot achieve our mandate as God's representation on earth. The arm of the flesh, no matter how articulate or gifted, is woefully inadequate to meet the demands of this needy generation. Only Christ in us, doing through us what He did on the earth in human form, can meet the challenge.

AS JANNES AND JAMBRES WITHSTOOD MOSES

The book of Exodus records that two men opposed Moses and Aaron through "magic arts" and divination. Interestingly, though the Old Testament does not give their names, Paul identifies them in his epistle to Timothy.

·   This example demonstrates how spiritual power was utilized to supernaturally withstand God's servant, Moses, in his commission and mandate. Nevertheless, God enabled him to walk in even greater measures of authority that made the counterfeit look foolish. Paul's account depicts the same spiritual dynamics for our day, recording that:

> Just as Jannes and Jambres opposed Moses, so these
> men also oppose the truth, men of depraved mind,
> rejected in regard to the faith. But they will not make
> further progress; for their folly will be obvious to all,
> just as Jannes' and Jambres' folly was also.
> —2 Timothy 3:8–9

People like Jannes and Jambres, who possess some measure of mystical virtue, will exist in our day. However, Jesus called those who enter the spiritual realm apart from Him robbers and thieves. Because the Lord is the source of true supernatural power, what we demonstrate in His name will be far superior, and make their folly obvious.

In a 1948 issue of *The Voice of Healing* magazine, Gordon Lindsay reported an incident during the inauguration of the Latter Rain healing movement that illustrates this confrontation. It transpired in a William Branham evangelistic and healing campaign in Portland, Oregon.

The first two days of the conference had gone extremely well. Testimonies of supernatural healing and mass salvations were abundant, and the services were filled to capacity. On the third night of the meetings, however, the conflict between light and darkness was pointedly illustrated. While Branham was ministering God's Word, a very large demon-possessed man, whom many recognized as one who frequently took pleasure in violently disrupting Christian meetings, burst through the back of the building and marched toward the platform shouting obscenities.

As two policemen moved to hinder him from his evil assignment, Branham requested they halt and let the man proceed. Once at the podium, the man released a startling array of profanities as a palpable "air" of evil spirits surrounded him and exuded from his countenance. Suddenly, though, when the man arrived within a few feet of God's servant, he could proceed no farther, for some unseen resistance arrested his advance and limited him to spitting upon the man of God and spewing more obscenities.

Clearly a showdown was happening between spirits of darkness and God's Spirit resting upon His servant. Gordon Lindsay recounts how William Branham confronted the man as David withstood Goliath. In a hushed tone, but with considerable authority, Branham rebuked the spirits and said, "Satan, because you have challenged the servant of God before this great congregation, you must bow before me. In the name of Jesus Christ, you shall fall at my feet."

Lindsay recorded that the man began to strain under the invisible force of the Holy Spirit as he gradually began to succumb to God's power superseding the demonic control in him. Beads of perspiration flowed down the man's face in his desperate effort to remain upright, until abruptly, the man who had so brazenly defied God's servant now slumped to the floor "in a sobbing and hysterical manner." Witnesses present testified that a wave of glory followed that would never be forgotten by those who experienced it.

Interestingly, Mrs. T. L. Osborn witnessed the entire episode from her balcony seat directly overlooking the podium and reported it to her husband, who returned the next evening to experience God's supernatural power firsthand. T. L. Osborn later reported that the Lord spoke to him that fateful evening in 1947 and said, "You can do that!" Osborn further testified that as he sat in William Branham's meeting, it was as though ten thousand voices spoke to him at once when God commissioned him into his healing and deliverance ministry. As a result, millions of people from India and other nations around the world have received the Lord Jesus Christ as their Savior and Healer through the ministry of T. L. Osborn and his wife, Daisy.

A GREATER COVENANT

The early Church demonstrated great spiritual activity as the seed generation; by necessity we warrant even more in the age of consummation. Paul's life following His conversion was filled with supernatural encounters, revelations, and visitations from the Lord. That must be our expectation as well! Haggai prophesied, "The glory of this latter house shall be greater than the former..." (Haggai 2:9)

In his letter to the Corinthians, Paul continued to use Moses as a standard because of the incredible privileges accorded him to know the Lord on a level few have ever attained. The Holy Spirit, through Paul's writings, challenges us to aspire to that prophetic destiny and more:

> But if the ministry of death, in letters engraved on
> stones, came with glory, so that the sons of Israel could
> not look intently at the face of Moses because of the
> glory of his face, fading as it was, how will the ministry

of the Spirit fail to be even more with glory?
                                        —2 Corinthians 3:7–8

If such glory and splendor accompanied the administration of God's law, how much more of His glory and miraculous dimension should we experience in the dispensation of God's Spirit? Furthermore, if Moses could encounter the Lord so intensely that his face required a veil through a covenant sealed with the blood of bulls and goats, how much more can we encounter His glory by the covenant sealed with the precious blood of Jesus Christ?

Our ultimate goal is not merely to discover angels and spiritual beings but to live in the Spirit's realm and encounter Jesus experientially and be transformed. John the Beloved articulated that it is not yet fully or clearly disclosed what we will be like following this age, nevertheless, when the Lord Jesus comes and manifests Himself at the end of the age, we will be like Him, for we will have seen Him as He really is.

> Beloved, now we are children of God; and it has not yet
> been revealed what we shall be, but we know that when
> He is revealed, we shall be like Him, for we shall see
> Him as He is. And everyone who has this hope in Him
> purifies himself, just as He is pure.
>   —1 John 3:2–3, NKJV

This truth of God's Word seems so fantastic it is difficult for our natural minds to grasp. Even so, the Bible foretells a generation of people will walk in this reality, and the spiritual signs indicate that we are indeed living at the very end of the age immediately preceding the Lord's return.

A TWENTIETH CENTURY PROTOTYPE

Spiritual tokens or prototypes of others who have found this place in God beckon us with their lives of victory and close encounters with the Living Savior. One such individual was John G. Lake. Lake lived during the early part of the twentieth century and stands out in his generation as a forerunner to the twenty-first century call to walk as "sons of the Kingdom."

Lake relates a specific personal encounter with the Lord that took place after several years of successful healing and evangelistic work. Although profound miracles were manifesting through him, a spiritual hunger still burned in his heart despite the ministry successes he was witnessing. Thus, in desperation to discover the experience with the Lord that would satisfy his longing heart, he initiated a nine month season of prayer and fasting. The Lord Jesus did not disappoint His loyal servant. One evening while visiting a believer's home for prayer, the tangible and visible glory of God pervaded the room, surrounding and filling him.

He encountered the Lord somewhat as Moses had and more. He now knew the reality of, "Christ in us, the hope of glory." The phenomenal fruit of a victorious life and profound ministry of Word and Spirit that overtook John G. Lake from this point on, validates the experience and encourages this generation to pursue the Lord with even more desperate hunger.

Lake later referred to this encounter in this way, "The glory of this experience remained in my soul. I found that my life began to manifest in the varied range of the gifts of the Spirit. Healings were of a more powerful order. My nature became so sensitized that I could lay my hands on any man or woman and tell what organ was diseased and to what extent."

John G. Lake went on to teach about this experience throughout the remainder of his life. He often expressed that this spiritual reality was what had made him a "Christ-man" and capable of demonstrating the radiant nature of a holy God.

We are not certain how much time we have, but we do know these prophetic promises are accessible; as the apostle recorded,

"Behold, a door standing open in heaven!" Angels working under the command of the Holy Spirit are released to help prepare us for this destiny. "Angels that gather" are presently empowered to remove both internal and external stumbling blocks placed to prohibit this calling. Recognizing this spiritual provision and strategy is the first step in its achievement.

GRACE FOR THE CROSSROAD

With every "fullness of time" juncture of Church history, the supernatural realm is opened to unveil God's plan. A heavenly host is being dispatched in large numbers to facilitate God's blueprint and work with the latter-day Church in clear and pronounced ways. Our job is to recognize this aspect of our spiritual legacy and to empower them with our prayers, proclamations, and prophetic decrees.

The angels are a consolidation of messengers of the Kingdom who are ministers of fire working cooperatively with ministering spirits who are like winds. The joining of fire with wind causes a great blaze. That is the desired effect of the spiritual host of Heaven assigned to labor with this generation in the consummation of God's heavenly design.

God's messengers will be empowered to extract from His Kingdom all causes of offense and arguments by which others are drawn into error or sin. When this happens in force, then the prophecy of Daniel will begin to be fulfilled (Daniel 12:3).The righteous, those who are upright and in right standing with God, will shine with the brilliance of the sun/Son in the Kingdom of their Father. That day is upon us!

When the heavens are opened another world comes into view, a dimension of God where believers in Christ are seated. From this place the angels descended on that fateful day and announced "glory to God in the highest," and only from this place can the ultimate commission originally stated in Genesis

1:26 be fulfilled. Here is where we are fashioned into the image and likeness of our Savior.

Angels are assigned to help us know and perpetually live in this realm. The Lord is releasing the wings of the wind to transport us from captivity into liberty and freedom. His angels are winds that fuel the flame of fire burning in the heart of his ministers. The Psalmist declared:

> He lays the beams of His upper chambers in the waters;
> He makes the clouds His chariot;
> He walks upon the wings of the wind;
> He makes the winds His messengers,
> Flaming fire His ministers.
>
> —Psalm 104:3–4

Great spiritual winds will come to lift us above the issues of this world as we learn to soar like eagles in the Spirit. This fresh wind will carry many to higher realms of revelation than they have known in the past and launch us into our end-time destiny.

My Eyes were Opened!

A fter a long day of flying and layovers, I was not expecting October 17, 2003, to be especially conducive to spiritual revelation. Needless to say, I was surprised and thrilled when my eyes were opened to the spiritual realm and I saw angels standing across the width of the church building that eventful evening.

My wife, Wanda, and I had been invited to participate in a dedication service at Vineyard Christian Fellowship in Albany, Oregon, a flourishing church that was expanding its facility to seat 1,500. We were joining many of our ministry friends, Bob Jones, Bobby Connor, Don and Christine Potter, and others who had already begun the dedication services on Thursday evening.

Because of a prior commitment on the East Coast, we arrived late Friday evening and had spent the entire day making connections in numerous airports. The day's journey had not promoted a very positive spiritual atmosphere and certainly did not prepare me for what transpired the moment I stepped into the sanctuary that evening.

HOLY SPIRIT SURPRISES

Very often we have the mistaken notion that only through extended periods of prayer and fasting will the Lord speak to us in clear and concise ways. Naturally, that is a good way to be positioned before God's Throne to hear from Him; but it is not the only way He speaks. Sometimes He chooses circumstances that may surprise us. For instance, the hardship and difficulty of John's excommunication to the island of Patmos made his visitations all the more meaningful. Clearly John's revelations arising from these circumstances are among the most profound ever entrusted to a human, but the principle is the same. Likewise, while tending sheep in the seclusion of a shepherd's life, Moses was forever transformed by a single supernatural encounter when the Angel of the Lord appeared to him as a flame of fire in the midst of a bush that was not consumed. That introduction to God's supernatural realm marked him for the remainder of his earthly days.

The Lord can speak to us in the midst of a storm, while performing mundane duties, in the turmoil of a great trial, or even after a very long day of airline travel. Whatever the surrounding circumstance, encounters with Heaven's host will always leave us changed and energized.

MY EYES WERE OPENED

The service had already begun when we arrived. Don Potter was leading worship, and the people were fully engaged in the service. Our escort opened the side door leading into the sanctuary, and I entered the new auditorium. Instantly, with that first step, I was seeing both the natural and spiritual realms at the same time. Although my natural eyes still viewed the people as they worshiped, my spiritual eyes were open to look into the Spirit's realm where, with open eyes, I observed angels standing from one corner of the building across the back to the other corner.

The angels appeared to be about six to seven feet tall, and wore white robes reaching to their feet. They stood approximately six feet apart, and some had golden belts that seemed to be made of a material resembling rope while others had golden sashes of the exact same color that draped across their chests. They were all attentively watching Don Potter as he was leading worship.

Their countenances were very compassionate and caring. Some I have witnessed from Heaven's host are fierce and overwhelming in appearance, but these angels seemed tender and loving. I initially struggled to find the right words to depict their demeanor.

My first question was "Who are they?" The Spirit provided the answer immediately and emphatically, "They are angels that gather." To my knowledge, I had never before heard that expression. "Angels that gather" was a fresh revelation to me.

As I took the seat next to the pastor I advised him that there were angels standing across the back of his church. He asked what kind of angels, to which I firmly and authoritatively replied, "They are angels that gather," although that phrase was made known to me only moments before.

Since first seeing these end-time emissaries that strategic evening, I have had the privilege of watching them co-labor with God's people on other occasions. It seems that we, as a generation, have crossed over a threshold in Heaven's timeline into a plan and strategy formulated in God's heart before time began. A specific company of Heaven's host has been dispatched to work with us in a unique way in order to achieve our latter-day mandate.

The Holy Spirit has broadened this generation's collective understanding considerably regarding His blueprint for this age and increased sensitivity to the spiritual realm. The admonition pointing to the emergence of a body of people, who are both Word and Spirit oriented, is genuinely in the process of being realized. Everything we experience in the Spirit will be grounded in God's Word, and all the promises of God's Word will be achieved in the Spirit.

A BIBLICAL WITNESS

That evening I asked the Lord for scriptural confirmation of what I had seen. I discovered the affirmation in Matthew 13. When Jesus interpreted the parable of the wheat and the tares, He was directly referring to the latter-day generation and clearly indicating the spiritual confrontation in the days immediately preceding His return. He said:

> "The one who sows the good seed is the Son of Man,
> and the field is the world; and as for the good seed,
> these are the sons of the kingdom; and the tares are the
> sons of the evil one; and the enemy who sowed them is
> the devil, and the harvest is the end of the age; and the
> reapers are angels.
>
> So just as the tares are gathered up and burned
> with fire, so shall it be at the end of the age. The Son
> of Man will send forth His angels, and they will gather
> out of His kingdom all stumbling blocks, and those
> who commit lawlessness, and will throw them into the
> furnace of fire; in that place there will be weeping and
> gnashing of teeth.
>
> Then THE RIGHTEOUS WILL SHINE FORTH AS
> THE SUN in the kingdom of their Father. He who has
> ears, let him hear."
>
> —Matthew 13:37–43

These are the primary components outlined in this passage that will set the stage for the end-time confrontation:

The Sower of Wheat—The Son of Man
The Sower of Tares—The Devil
The Field—The World
The Good Seed—Sons of the Kingdom

The Tares—Sons of the wicked one
The Harvest—The End of the Age
The Reapers—Angels That Gather

The Bible plainly states that the field the Lord has sown good seed into, is the world. The One who sows the good seed is the Son of Man, and the seed He imparts will result in a harvest field of people like Himself. Consequently, we know with certainty who we are called to be in this generation—sons of the Kingdom. Furthermore, this company must be on the earth before His return because He has promised to harvest them and use a specially equipped host of angels in this process—"angels that gather."

The end-of-the-age will be the ultimate harvest. One thing we know concerning the Lord—He will not harvest something unless it is mature. Souls, promises, commissions, and destinies will all be reaped as seeds of light and darkness alike are accelerating into maturity.

A cursory examination of media headlines serves to validate the burgeoning darkness overshadowing many of this generation. Fortunately, we have God's undeniable promise that His "sons of the Kingdom" will also progress to their full maturity and overcome the darkness.

Meanwhile, Jesus guarantees us supernatural assistance in this task by the heavenly host specifically prepared and assigned for this epic season. If we are radically pursuing God, He had to first spark that movement within us. Jesus taught that no one comes to Him unless they are first drawn by the Father through the Spirit's influence and aid (John 6:44). Therefore, the Lord will certainly grant us the grace we need to overcome, and provide a host of ministering spirits to assist in this struggle. "Angels that gather" will not only collect the wheat into the barn, but also remove stumbling blocks to our ultimate destiny.

REMOVING STUMBLING BLOCKS

Since first seeing the "angels that gather" in 2003, I have often sensed their presence or visibly recognized their activity in numerous meetings we have conducted throughout the U.S. and abroad. I have noticed that a predominant assignment given to them is to assist believers by extracting their stumbling blocks and anything offensive to the Lord. The Lord declared:

> "The Son of Man will send forth His angels, and they
> will gather out of His kingdom all stumbling blocks,
> and those who commit lawlessness..."
> —Matthew 13:41

As the Son of Man, the Lord will dispatch angels equipped with the necessary qualities to gather obstacles to destiny out of His Kingdom and expunge spiritual error leading to lawlessness. A. W. Tozer states in his book *The Pursuit of God*, "Seeking truth and seeking God is one and the same thing." Our hearts and motives must be pure before God if we are to walk in the high calling set apart for us.

The Holy Spirit once told me, "If you will allow Me to remove the stumbling blocks within you, I will then remove the ones before you." We often believe it is the enemy withstanding us when perhaps it is the Lord.

God sometimes allows hindrances in ministry growth in order to accomplish a work within us that facilitates a much deeper communion with Him and greater personal anointing. Before the Lord can remove the wicked from among the righteous as promised, He must first remove wickedness from within the hearts of the righteous.

A stumbling block can be defined as anything that stands in the way of intimate relationship with Him. On one occasion a rich young man approached Jesus and asked what he must do to become a disciple. For him, the requirement was to relinquish his riches and give to the poor. His wealth was his stumbling block.

Wealth is not always a stumbling block, but it can be. Interestingly, there were many other wealthy people who did not seem to have the same requirement placed upon them. The Lord looks into the fabric of our motives to determine our issues. Actually, He is the only one capable of judging what truly constitutes a stumbling block within each of us as individuals.

The need for this work of God's Spirit is becoming more and more apparent as media headlines continue to feature prominent spiritual leaders who have fallen into snares of darkness. We all stand entirely by God's grace and by His favor alone are we set free from the tares in our souls before the great confrontation between light and darkness reaches its pinnacle.

Scripture emphasizes that as men and women of God, the Kingdom exists within us.

> ...The kingdom of God does not come with observation; nor will they say, 'See here!' or 'See there!' For indeed, the kingdom of God is within you.
> — Luke 17:20–21, NKJV

I once was transported to a heavenly operating table where spiritual surgery is performed. In this place the Great Physician diagnoses and treats our carnality and inhibitions while simultaneously His Spirit, assisted by "angels that gather," excise from our Kingdom existence past failures, spiritual and emotional wounds, debilitating fears, and various soulish strongholds and dominions thwarting our destinies. Our part is to insist upon and yield to this process.

This preparatory grooming must be performed within each of us to function fruitfully in His Kingdom. God's dealings always start first in His own house. Once it has progressed, the righteous will begin to shine like the sun in the Father's Kingdom and all nations will be drawn to our light.

THE MINISTRY OF GATHERING
The Lord has deposited into this world Kingdom seeds to produce sons and daughters who manifest on earth what He did. Unfortunately, Satan has sown unholy seeds of tares into the same field to yield sons of the evil one (Matthew 13:38). Some Bible versions translate tare as darnel, which is a weed closely resembling wheat but without the seeds of life that produces wheat.

Generally, the only time wheat can be distinguished from tares is during harvesttime. Jesus warns us that a spirit will so closely counterfeit God's Spirit as to deceive the very elect if possible (Matthew 24:24). However, the difference between them will be clearly detected when the wheat becomes mature and carries seeds of life, causing it to bow over, while the tares remain stiff and unyielding.

The final harvest is the consummation of the ages in which reapers, or angels, will be released to co-labor with us in the fields of humanity. Not only will the wheat be gathered into the barns, but the darnel will be gathered to be burned. For this unique day in human history and closure of the age, the Lord promised to send specially prepared gathering angels to cooperate in this responsibility.

The introductory work of these angels has already been a tremendous blessing, although sometimes it may seem harsh and difficult. They have been working to gather the tare nature from within believers. The end result of this pruning and extraction will be the emergence of "sons of the Kingdom" operating with true spiritual authority and power to sustain the coming outpouring.

Carefully analyzing past revivals and the demonic snares they confronted, help us identify obstacles to sustaining our day of visitation. God's great grace is presently being offered so that we can be free from ambition, greed, and pride. These and other diabolical influences have consistently raised their ugly heads throughout church history to undermine the full release of God's presence among His people.

When we surrender to the work of God's Spirit, we will experience a clear and distinct awareness of His goodness and glory. The Holy Spirit is always among us; however, the experiential awareness of His abiding presence is what will earmark "sons of the Kingdom."

The Lord promised if we cooperate with Him in loving obedience, He would manifest Himself to us and allow us to live in His radiant presence. If Moses, through the Old Covenant experienced His presence with the mere residue of God's glory requiring a veil to cover his face, how much more can we, partakers of the new covenant sealed by the blood of Jesus, expect to experience and dwell in His manifest presence?

SPIRITUAL PROTOTYPES

The twentieth century produced a number of individuals who achieved a place as spiritual prototypes representing God. They did this, not by fleshly works and human striving, but by yielding to the Holy Spirit and continuing to press in to Him for the prize of this high calling.

Many of these men and women were well known in public ministry, such as William Branham, Maria Woodworth-Etter, Kathryn Kuhlman, and John G. Lake, while others were hidden and never recognized on earth but were certainly well known in Heaven.

A consistent thread of truth is apparent with each forerunner. They became partakers of the Lord's divine nature and lived in a breakthrough relationship with Him. These qualities will typify the end-time company. Their example will pave the way for many to follow in this generation.

Since the early '90s, God's Spirit has been speaking to Wanda and me about this reality. On August 11, 1995, a beautiful white dove landed on our balcony and remained. From that time forward the Lord has been speaking to us about the Dove Company who will emerge in this generation as "sons of the Kingdom." Their communion and intimacy with the Lord will be intense, and the powerful authority they walk in will provoke this generation. Many of the spiritual pioneers who foresaw this day also prophesied the spiritual opportunity this army would have with the Lord.

The Dove Company will be a body of people upon whom the Holy Spirit descends and remains. Jesus experienced that same reality that fateful day at the Jordan River. The heavens opened and the Holy Spirit descended as the appearance of a dove and remained to empower Him with His presence (Matthew 3:16).

The dove is a symbol of purity, the Holy Spirit, and the adoption of sonship. The Dove Company will be an emblem of the mature bride without spot or wrinkle who makes herself ready and lives in union with her Beloved.

Not only do some figures in modern Church history provide intimations of this truth, but even others who lived through the Dark Ages recognized this reality. The fourteenth century mystic, St. Catherine of Sienna, foresaw this day. Her life of prayer and devotion yielded numerous well-documented visions and revelations from the Lord. She was often "caught up" in the Spirit and foretold numerous future events including the Reformation and revivals closely resembling our nation's Latter Rain healing movement. But, most importantly, she foresaw the beautiful Bride of Christ arising in the last days in garments of holiness and purity upon whom the glory of God would descend and fill the earth. That is the hour in which we are now living.

LIVING WITHOUT COMPROMISE

John G. Lake was also familiar with such moves of the Spirit and recognized firsthand the refining work necessary to carry them. After birthing multiple apostolic churches in South Africa, this man of God returned to Spokane, Washington, to establish numerous houses of healing. Thousands who were sick and dying experienced God's healing power through his ministry and the Northwest was once considered our nation's healthiest region because of him. During the early twentieth century, this inspired vessel recorded more than one hundred thousand documented cases of supernatural healing.

Subsequently, John G. Lake shared this message in March 1916:

> "Think not to come within the court of God with stain upon thy garments. Think not that Heaven can smile upon a nature fouled through evil contact. Think not that Christ can dwell in temples seared by flames of hate. No! The heart of man must first be purged by holy fire and washed from every stain by cleansing blood. Know ye that he whose nature is akin to God's must feel the purging power of Christ within?"

He continued:

> "He who would understand the ways of God must trust the Spirit's power to guide and keep; he who would tread the paths where angels tread, himself must realize seraphic purity. Such is the nature of God; such is the working of the Spirit's power; such is the attainment of him who overcomes. In him the joy and power of God shall be; through him the healing streams of life shall flow; to him Heaven's gates are opened wide; in him the

Kingdom is revealed."

THE TARES OF OUR SOUL
Several years ago, I went through a difficult season that illustrates this principle. This trying time followed the release of several very encouraging prophetic words for our ministry through several of our highly regarded and respected prophetic friends. These words were regarding my and Wanda's calling and commission as well as many of our hearts' secret desires.

During this troublesome time, every base and carnal influence seemed to flash to the forefront of my mind, consuming my every thought and imagination. Overwhelming feelings of discouragement, rejection, anger, and disappointment began to surface, making it difficult to pray or even study the Bible.

Nothing I tried to conquer this attack seemed to work.   I employed every teaching I had assimilated over the years to overcome demonic assaults on our walk. I rebuked everything oppressing my mind. I recited the Scriptures just as I had learned and called upon the Lord to defend me against what I perceived as an all-out enemy barrage. When none of these techniques availed, I placed a desperate call to our prophetic friend Bob Jones.

When he answered, I realized he had been waiting for my call. The Lord had already informed him about the dilemma I was facing. When he shared the revelation he had received from the Holy Spirit, I was somewhat surprised and dismayed. He told me he had seen in a vision the Lord, "pouring water on the tares of my soul." What an unusual expression!

The Lord was actually causing seeds of corruption that existed within my soul to germinate and bud so they could be exposed and dealt with. Bob advised, "The tares of your soul are blossoming; the Lord is sending the angels to gather them and remove them by the roots to be burned."

The Lord was causing the base nature to begin to blossom so I would call upon His mercy and grace for their removal. The merger of the Word and the Spirit provided the essential ingredients for the cleansing process to claim divine life and illumination within my soul.

The Holy Spirit had to actively summon these issues to the surface in order for me to recognize them and engage divine aid to appropriately deal with them. Many times, carnal issues remain hidden deep within our souls only to be exploited by our adversary at the most opportune time. At the pinnacle of our ministry, he strives to shipwreck the calling and anointing accorded for a divine purpose.

The mere recital of Scriptures was not sufficient. This spiritual surgery required the Spirit's revelatory anointing to quicken and make alive the Word of Truth necessary to replace seeds of corruption with the dominion of His divine attributes.

Bob exhorted, "Do not faint; the first harvest is at hand." That seemed both good and bad news to me: good in that these oppressive and debilitating feelings would be extracted, but bad in so far as FIRST harvest indicated others would follow. In reality, this was actually good news also, because our hearts truly desire to be thoroughly purged of the seeds of corruption that veil and separates us from the Lord and the intimate walk with Him we desperately seek.

SUSTAINED VISION

When we make the Lord Jesus our refuge, it paves the way for Him to release our inheritance and invite us into a holy place with Him. The prophet Isaiah foretold this reality saying:

"Build up, build up, prepare the way,
Remove every obstacle out of the way of
My people."
For thus says the high and exalted One

Who lives forever, whose name is Holy,
"I dwell on a high and holy place,
And also with the contrite and lowly of spirit
In order to revive the spirit of the lowly
And to revive the heart of the contrite."
—Isaiah 57:14–15

We are presently living at a threshold of divine destiny and the Lord's manifest presence unlike anything any other generation has ever known. Focusing on crossing into this offering will motivate us to move beyond nominal Christianity into full maturity.

Throughout the Body of Christ, believers have shared with us how the Lord has been putting His finger on specific issues and strongholds in their lives. By God's grace, they are allowing the Holy Spirit to eradicate carnality, false ambition, and spiritual sinkholes of deception.

History has shown that almost every revival ended because worldly qualities overtook the hearts of key leaders entrusted with the revival's stewardship. Extraordinary opportunity is being offered to conquer this frailty so we can sustain God's visitation without it destroying our wineskins and losing His wine.

Therefore, the first place the "angels that gather" have been busy working is within you and me by removing the tares of our souls, those seeds of corruption imparted to us in our mother's womb. The prophet David recognized this in his own life saying:

Behold, I was brought forth in iniquity,
And in sin my mother conceived me.
Behold, You desire truth in the innermost being,
And in the hidden part You will make me know
  wisdom.
—Psalm 51:5–6

This host has been working under the jurisdiction of God's Spirit to help identify and extract the tare nature within us. Although we can be born again with Heaven as our future home, we can still struggle with issues of rejection, anger, lust, ambition, and other carnal entanglements. Paul's epistles make this abundantly clear! Even so, the Lord has already prophesied of mature sons and daughters of His Kingdom on the earth at the end of the age. They will constitute a company of those who overcome the spirit of this world and live victoriously in incredible relationship with Him, displaying extraordinary power and authority to achieve His mandate.

Once the work of extraction is complete, then the gathering angels will co-labor with us to bring a harvest of souls into God's Kingdom and into their personal destinies. They work first within us to prepare us, then with us to gather the harvest.

THREE SNAKES

I once viewed this reality in a vision that was like a living panorama. Power lines, similar to those connected to the electric power poles surrounding our cities, appeared. However, in this setting, they were not connected to an earthly power plant, but to the true source of all power in Heaven.

I noticed that God's power was not flowing freely because the power lines were connected to transformers inadequately equipped to handle the tremendous power generated from the source. These transformers were symbolic of latter-day Christians. I knew that our internal circuitry had to be totally reworked in order for us to accommodate God's level of power without it short-circuiting and blowing up. Jesus related this principle:

> And no one puts new wine into old wineskins;
> otherwise the new wine will burst the skins and it will
> be spilled out, and the skins will be ruined. But new

wine must be put into fresh wineskins.

—Luke 5:37–38

I was curious and wondered why the transformers were so inadequate to handle the level of power that needed to flow through them. I then watched as my own mother appeared in the vision and walked over to one of the transformers. Suddenly, I was the actual transformer. She opened the transformer door, and I watched as she deposited three small green serpents in me. These three serpents would not allow the full measure of power that needed to flow and be released.

I immediately understood what these three serpents represented and where they were identified in Scripture.

For all that is in the world, the lust of the flesh and the lust of the eyes and the boastful pride of life, is not from the Father, but is from the world.

—1 John 2:16

The three serpents deposited in us in our mother's womb are:

The Lust of the Flesh
The Lust of the Eyes
The Boastful Pride of Life

In the vision, the Lord allowed me to reach within my own soul to extract these three serpents. They appeared docile and friendly until I made my intent to destroy them known. I immediately threw them into a fiery altar; to say their reaction was violent would be an understatement. They frantically tried to escape the fire and attack me. I had to stand at the altar with a rod of authority to force them to remain there until they were consumed.

The interpretation of this vision is not complicated. My mother was representative of the analogy David shared in Psalm 51. In sin are we conceived in our mother's womb with a fallen nature requiring God's redemptive work through the blood of Jesus Christ and the refinement of His Spirit.

When we are born again our spirit is regenerated and immediately enters into conflict with our soul, which comprises our mind, will, and emotions. That is the very struggle Paul identified in Romans 7:19: The thing that he wants to do he does not do and the thing that he does not want to do is what he is compelled to do. Such is the clash between these two natures.

By God's grace we are being given the opportunity to have these three fallen natures and all their defiling attributes extracted from our souls. That is how we are transformed from glory to glory and begin to reflect the Lord's image. Only then will the full measure of God's power flow through us to reach our generation. This process is not painless, but it must be pursued with radical abandonment despite how violently our flesh rebels.

The good news is the Lord has provided the power of His blood and the working of His Spirit to usher us through. Jesus declared that He is sending angels to gather every stumbling block and offensive quality out of His Kingdom. Our reward for undergoing this transformative process is a place of fellowship with Him that molds us into pure mirrors of His image and powerful "sons of the Kingdom."

This biblical principle is not new; it is just receiving fresh attention from God's Spirit as a present-day reality. One of the earliest pioneers for this truth was Ethan O. Allen, considered the father of the mid-nineteenth century American healing movement.

In 1846 he became the first member of that movement to embrace the doctrine of Christian perfection along with divine healing.

Many forerunners promoted the truth restored in Methodism that Christ's atonement avails not only for justification, but also for the purification of the sinful human nature. When this cleansing is accomplished we will become more adequately qualified to participate in the coming harvest. Excellence of character is a prerequisite for being endowed with the level of God's authority and anointing essential in this age. And by this anointing and authority we will reap a harvest of harvesters who will be the laborers in the great harvest.

CHAPTER

2

Gather
and Guard

One of the Lord's most wonderful assurances resounded through the prophet Jeremiah—God has a plan! Not only does He have an engineered design fully backed by His Kingdom, but it is intended for our welfare and affords us hope for the future, rather than a dismal end. The Lord said:

> For I know the thoughts and plans that I have for you,
> says the Lord, thoughts and plans for welfare and peace
> and not for evil, to give you hope in your final outcome.
> —Jeremiah 29:11, AMP

I had a spiritual dream illustrating this principle. I saw a thought materializing from God's heart and given birth. At first the thought had the appearance of an immature embryo, but it quickly took on shape and form and became a living display of His heart.

We have the prophetic assurance that God has expectations and designs for our welfare and not our misfortune. The Holy

Spirit searches the depths of God (1 Corinthians 2:10) and, by the Spirit of Revelation, gives articulation to His thoughts and ways—this is what it means to access the mind of Christ.

Thoughts from the mind of Christ express His counsel and purpose for this generation and the deposit of His Spirit to accomplish the heavenly design. These plans cannot be appropriated through natural wisdom or by carnal human reasoning; rather, these designs can only be revealed to His people by the Holy Spirit. I inherently knew the visual image in my dream represented something new and fresh being birthed directly from God's heart.

Very often individuals or fellowships seek a word from the Lord. A word is a thought that has been given expression. God has preserved in His heart something unique and creative for this age that will consolidate spiritual thoughts with spiritual language.

It is His good pleasure to grant us glimpses into His divine strategies and articulate plans for this generation so we can position ourselves to cooperate more fully with Him.

LIGHT VERSUS DARKNESS

During one revelatory experience, I found myself on a battlefield preparing to participate in a conflict between the armies of light and darkness. Each army was in battle array, aligned and facing one another, waiting for the signal to initiate the struggle. When the battle ensued the armies converged with all the sounds and imagery normally associated with a confrontation of this nature. Symbolically, it seemed as though a record or score were being kept between the two armies as the conflict heightened.

At certain junctures the army of darkness would press the army of light and the score would reflect that advance in much the same way that a sporting event would keep score. Then, the army of light would rally and begin to take ground against darkness and the scoreboard would likewise reflect that change.

I realized I was experiencing a visionary parable epitomizing the spiritual conflict that has been raging throughout Church history, as the ebb and flow of spiritual awakening was recorded. There were times of tremendous spiritual release from God's throne resulting in revival and restoration, as though a spirit of grace were released to His people and the battle escalated to the advantage of the army of light.

Then, at other times, demonic hordes would unleash treacherous political, religious, and controlling spirits to derail the flow of God's Spirit in the hearts of the people involved. These strongholds then paved the way for ambition, greed, sexual sin, and other snares to cause the army of darkness to seemingly prevail for a season, and the revival would be lost. Simple examination of Church history delineates these times and seasons.

On several occasions I have been allowed access to heavenly places to view these evil spirits' realm, observing their habitats and hideous appearances. The more appealing these demonic forces are to our carnal nature, the more detestable they appear in the spiritual realm. I have been allowed to see the spirits of perversion and homosexuality that are prevalent in our world today.

If people could only see how grotesque and repulsive they truly appear we would be far less susceptible to their snares. Interestingly, the spirit of homosexuality is not only morbid in appearance, but also exudes an extremely violent disposition, as though it desires to devour everything it comes in contact with. That was somewhat surprising to me when the Lord allowed me to see its operation.

Victorious ones in our generation must learn to overcome evil devices to march forward into our high calling. What is coming now is to be perpetuated. It is not to be a short seasonal expression of God's anointing but His lasting presence.

TIME IS RUNNING OUT

I was allowed in my "battlefield" experience to observe this vacillating battle transition take place many times, with the lead changing on numerous occasions, until the clock indicated that "time was running out."

With only seconds remaining in the confrontation, the army of darkness was leading on the scoreboard. They rallied all their strength for one final assault in their attempt to totally overrun the army of light. As God's army observed the scoreboard and discovered only seconds remaining, we called upon the Lord with all our strength. When we did, from behind us came shouts of "Grace, grace." In an unprecedented release of divine grace, the Lord intervened on our behalf, allowing us to mount a formidable assault and achieve the ultimate victory as "time" ran out.

The victory was decisive, and jubilant celebration erupted among those participating in the army of light. As we were enjoying the Lord's incredible grace and the victory He had given, I peered at the scoreboard. To my surprise and slight dismay, I discovered the score read 41–41. The victory was sure and the celebration was evident, so I knew it was not a tie. A voice said, "Genesis 41:41." I understood this spiritual parable could be interpreted from this passage.

> Pharaoh said to Joseph, "See, I have set you over all the
> land of Egypt." Then Pharaoh took off his signet ring
> from his hand and put it on Joseph's hand, and clothed
> him in garments of fine linen and put the gold necklace
> around his neck.
> —Genesis 41:41–42

As I began to meditate on this notable Scripture and Joseph's promotion from dungeon to throne in a single day, the Lord quickened significant truths to me, regarding our calling as the apostolic Church. This revelatory experience showed that we had received God's grace to overcome the enemy resistance attempting to prohibit the birthing of this significant end-time ministry.

I had never before recognized that the promised Joseph anointing entailed much more than providing a source of plenty in time of famine. Included in this important calling and commission is an apostolic mantle with bold spiritual authority and godly character.

THREEFOLD JOSEPH ANOINTING

The incipient "Joseph" ministry involves much more than providing resources in time of deficiency; the true Joseph ministry is a threefold anointing typified in Genesis 41:42.

In one day Joseph was elevated from prison to palace. He went from garments of slavery to royal attire. First he received the signet ring, illustrating the spiritual authority that will emerge in the "Joseph" company. The ring of authority proclaimed that Joseph had the king's full endorsement and influence and answered only to the king.

Secondly, Joseph was dressed in linen garments, prophetically depicting the priesthood of the Lord—clothed in purity and Christ's nature. The priestly linen garments of His divine character and nature will replace our filthy garments of unrighteousness; they are the impartation of His heart. The Joseph Company will be trustworthy stewards of the sevenfold Spirit of God that rested upon Jesus. This prominent ministry will require great meekness of heart because of the natural and spiritual resources entrusted to them.

Finally, Joseph received a gold chain, exemplifying the prosperity that will be entrusted to this company. God's purposes will demand abundant resources to fully accomplish end-time ministry and fulfill God's will on earth. These resources will include places of refuge and provision for those who will be persecuted, as well as for those displaced by the extreme natural disasters and military confrontations taking place.

JOSEPH—A TYPE OF CHRIST

Since my battlefield encounter, the Holy Spirit has progressively unveiled critical understanding of this passage as it pertains to His desire for this season. Much has been written and spoken about Joseph ministries as they relate to an emerging company of entrepreneurs who will have key roles in providing needed resources for the harvest.

The Bible also illustrates Joseph as a perfect type of Christ, for many parallels in Joseph's life highlight meaningful attributes in Jesus' life and ministry.

JOSEPH	JESUS
Greatly loved by his father Israel (Genesis 37:3)	This is my beloved Son in whom I delight (Matthew 3:17)
Sent by his father to his brothers (Genesis 37:13)	Not ashamed to call us brethren (Hebrews 2:11)
Sent by his father to shepherd his sheep (Genesis 37:2)	The Good Shepherd who lays down His life for the sheep (John 10:11)
Hated by his brothers though he came to them peaceably (Genesis 37:4)	His brothers did not believe, adhere to, or trust Him (John 7:5)
His brothers plotted to kill him (Genesis 37:20)	They plotted together how they might put Him to death (John 11:53)
Tempted to sin (Genesis 39:7)	Tempted by the devil (Matthew 4:1)
Sent into the land of Egypt (Genesis 37:25)	Out of Egypt have I called My Son (Matthew 2:15)

Stripped of his garment (Genesis 37:23)	They took His garments (John 19:23)
Sold in exchange for 20 pieces of silver (Genesis 37:28)	Betrayed for 30 pieces of silver (Matthew 26:15)
Accused falsely by another (Genesis 39:16–18)	False witnesses testified against Him (Matthew 26:59)
One prisoner preserved, the other lost (Genesis 40:2–3)	One thief preserved, the other lost (Luke 23:32)
Began serving pharaoh at thirty years of age (Genesis 41: 46)	Began His public ministry at age thirty (Luke 3:23)
Took a bride from among the Egyptians (Genesis 41:45)	A bride from among the Gentiles (2 Corinthians 11:2)
First hid his identity from his brothers (Genesis 42:7)	Unrecognized by His Jewish brethren at His first appearing (John 12:37–40)
Forgave his brothers who rejected him (Genesis 45:1–15)	Father forgive them (Luke 23:34)
What was intended for evil God meant for good (Genesis 50:20)	The enemy didn't know God's mystery (1 Corinthians 2:7–8)

A BLUEPRINT FOR HARVEST

Joseph represented Christ's life. He possessed supernatural insight into God's plan though no human was capable of discerning it. Only God, from His eternal perspective, could meticulously orchestrate Joseph's steps to place him squarely in the right place at precisely the designated moment in human history to preserve a generation.

These events provided a prophetic shadow of the coming Messiah. The Holy Spirit has been granting added revelation concerning these patterns in Joseph's life as a blueprint for the present-day harvest.

Joseph had ascended to the right hand of Pharaoh and received all authority in the land of Egypt. He then facilitated the perfect

strategy: empowering Egypt not only to survive the coming
judgments but to flourish during them. He said:

> Now let Pharaoh look for a man discerning and wise,
> and set him over the land of Egypt. Let Pharaoh take
> action to appoint overseers in charge of the land,
> and let him exact a fifth of the produce of the land
> of Egypt in the seven years of abundance. Then let
> them gather all the food of these good years that are
> coming, and store up the grain for food in the cities
> under Pharaoh's authority, and let them guard it. Let
> the food become as a reserve for the land for the seven
> years of famine which will occur in the land of Egypt,
> so that the land will not perish during the famine.
> —Genesis 41:33–36

These are the present day components of Joseph's insight:

Wise and Discerning Leader—The Holy Spirit
Overseers—Fivefold leadership with spiritual authority
Storehouses—Regions for harvest and schools of ministry
Mandate—*Gather and guard* a harvest of wheat
Authority—Go into the fields surrounding the storehouse
   with authority to claim one in five

A BLUEPRINT TO FLOURISH

Clearly the Lord is doing many things in the earth today. Even so,
I believe a portion of Heaven's strategy is to follow this pattern
orchestrated by Joseph that successfully preserved a generation
and empowered a nation.

The Holy Spirit is presently working to identify storehouses
and appoint overseers with spiritual authority to reap a harvest
of one in five, in the same way Joseph commanded that twenty

percent of Egypt's wheat be designated for Pharaoh. A body of people who have been in Heaven's furnace and allowed Him to remove tares of the soul that have been stumbling blocks to their personal destinies will implement His plan.

> **Storehouses**—Cities and regions of great spiritual light that will be havens of rest and empowerment for God's people; numerous churches or ministries can operate within these regions.
>
> **Overseers**—Men and women charged with the responsibility and necessary authority to gather and guard the wheat (people) until the appointed time.
>
> **Harvest Fields**—The population of people who reside within a specific geographical radius of storehouses.
>
> **Wheat**—The "sons of the Kingdom" being groomed and prepared for the great harvest that is to come.

There are corporate bodies currently being commissioned as storehouses with delegated divine authority to function as gathering places for a firstfruits harvest of laborers for the great harvest. It will be a harvest of harvesters. Jesus said:

> The harvest is plentiful, but the laborers are few;
> therefore beseech the Lord of the harvest to send out
> laborers into His harvest.
> —Luke 10:2

We are promised "angels that gather" to co-labor with us in this mandate. As the overseers appropriate their spiritual authority through prayer, praise, and prophetic proclamations, these angels are energized and released into the purpose for which they were created—to gather future laborers for the great harvest.

Our "Joseph" has been given all authority in Heaven and

earth. He is now implementing a plan for this generation's salvation and searches the land on a quest to produce faithful overseers and identify regions as storehouses. He is ardently endeavoring to prepare a body of people to whom He can impart spiritual authority as Joseph did the overseers of Egypt.

FUNCTION OF OVERSEERS

The overseers will delegate their spiritual authority in the wheat fields surrounding the storehouses through prayer, praise, and prophetic decrees to bring in an allotted harvest. Strategic cities and regions are being prepared as storehouses to implement worship and ministry in the order of David's Tabernacle to facilitate this plan.

No power in the realms of darkness will be able to withstand this commission. As it was in the days of Joseph, submission to this blueprint is mandatory. The powers of darkness may attempt to thwart this divine plan, but God's purpose will be accomplished and the Lord will have His harvest. The enemy must relinquish this harvest, because Heaven's authority will supersede the spirit of this world. This generation will yield its harvest to the power of Jesus' blood. All Heaven affirms:

> "Worthy are You to take the book and to break its seals;
> for You were slain, and purchased for God with Your
> blood men from every tribe and tongue and people
> and nation. You have made them to be a kingdom and
> priests to our God; and they will reign upon the earth."
> —Revelation 5:9–10

We are at a "fullness of time" juncture; divine destiny shall be fulfilled. There is a body of people whose spiritual DNA has been specially crafted for this hour. Many laborers may come from difficult and diverse conditions, but grace will be given to them, awakening them to this cause. The seals on the Book of Redemption are opened and embodied in a company of overcomers who cohesively align with Heaven's host to fully appropriate the power of Jesus' blood to claim a spiritual harvest.

God's Word predicts very dark days for the end-of-time generation, yet despite this, it will be the time when God's people, who walk with Him in fellowship and authority, will be unveiled—in fact, it will be our greatest hour. As Zechariah predicted, "But at evening time it shall happen that it will be light"(Zechariah 14:7, NKJV).

A "famine" is arising in the land for hope, peace, and the true hearing of God's Word—that time will mark the unleashing of God's people who possess all the above and more. The storehouses will be opened and an army of radical believers will march forth in great faith and victory, as Joel predicted:

> "Then I will make up to you for the years
> That the swarming locust has eaten,
> The creeping locust, the stripping locust and the
>   gnawing locust,
> My great army which I sent among you.
> You will have plenty to eat and be satisfied
> And praise the name of the LORD your God,
> Who has dealt wondrously with you;
> Then My people will never be put to shame."
> —Joel 2:25–26

Presently, the masses are not yet hungry enough for this company to be released. Our present strategy is to gather the laborers into the barns for a season of accelerated education and maturity. At a pivotal moment these labors shall be released into the wheat fields of humanity for the great harvest. Right now we are poised for the harvest of harvesters, for the great harvest is still to come.

Joseph ordered the overseers to guard the wheat until the seven years of plenty had finished. The storehouses didn't need to open when everyone else enjoyed abundant wheat. Instead, this portion was reserved for the season of hardship.

When that time arrived, Egypt became the most powerful nation on the face of the earth. From around the world nations poured into Egypt and gave all they had to acquire wheat. It is about to get very dark in the world. When we are the only sources of true spiritual life with genuine answers for difficult problems, then the nations of the earth will be drawn to receive the Lord and His sustenance.

Initially, there must be a firstfruits harvest of laborers for the great harvest, and then the global harvest will follow. Depending upon their maturity and faithful stewardship, overseers will be afforded varying ranges and degrees of authority to call in the laborers. Some will command a radius of authority extending 250 miles to convene the one in five.

A TOKEN OF VICTORY

When I first communicated this vision in a meeting, the Lord provided a wonderful affirmation of its present pertinence. An associate pastor with one of the churches cooperating in the meeting contacted me about two weeks after the conference and related his testimony of what transpired after he heard this message and released his faith into it for a harvest. Besides being an associate pastor, he also happened to be a basketball coach at a local high school and had been sharing the gospel with his fifteen players in hopes of positively impacting their lives.

He told me he had seen no fruit from his efforts but knew he was sowing Kingdom seeds nonetheless. Then, within days of praying for the Lord of the Harvest to release "angels that gather," a knock resounded at his front door. Surprisingly, three of his players had come to inquire about Jesus and how they might be saved.

Just as the overseers were given authority to "exact a fifth of the produce of the land," exactly one in five students responded. He explained that there was nothing to cause this sudden change of heart in these young men except the Lord giving this as a token to build faith in this divine strategy.

On another occasion a pastor in the Pacific Northwest heard me preach this message at the close of a conference. As a result, before he and the others with him left to return home that evening, they beseeched God to release and empower the "angels that gather." The next morning at his Sunday service he noticed eighteen people who had never attended his church before. There was no other explanation for this increase except for the "angels that gather."

People have captured this revelation and are imploring the Lord to release "angels that gather" in order to facilitate dispensing Kingdom revelation in their churches and communities. They are entreating the Lord to send His grace to remove stumbling blocks that have kept them from their destinies, and spirits of depression, oppression, and shame are being extracted.

THE EXAMPLE OF PAUL

Paul was a commissioned officer who functioned as a spiritual overseer. He was given a sealed affidavit from Heaven granting him authority to gather the firstfruits harvest of his day. Our latter-day company will likewise have authority to proclaim God's Kingdom message and empower angels to labor with us to gather a harvest of souls that will be guarded and equipped for the next major move of God's Spirit.

The Bible records prophets and teachers at Antioch were advised by the Holy Spirit to set apart Paul and Barnabas for a unique work. They were commissioned and launched into an apostolic ministry with divine authority and supernatural empowerment. The same model operates for twenty-first century leaders anointed with God's Spirit as overseers. Acts 13 confirms that:

> While they were ministering to the Lord and fasting, the Holy Spirit said, "Set apart for Me Barnabas and Saul for the work to which I have called them." Then, when they had fasted and prayed and laid their hands on them, they sent them away. So, being sent out by the Holy Spirit, they went…
>
> —Acts 13:2–4

Paul's life demonstrates forerunner events that apply in our generation.

FOURFOLD APOSTOLIC MANDATE

True apostolic leadership will be commissioned with a fourfold mandate similar to the apostle Paul's. The Lord sent one of His cherished friends, Ananias, to release a prophetic commission to the just converted Saul of Tarsus. Ananias charged Paul with four specific admonitions that overshadowed the remainder of his life—the same ones that will characterize apostolic leaders of our day as well. The Scripture states:

> A certain Ananias, a man who was devout by the standard of the Law, and well spoken of by all the Jews who lived there, came to me, and standing near said to me, "Brother Saul, receive your sight!" And at that very time I looked up at him. And he said, "The God of our fathers has appointed you to know His will and to see the Righteous One and to hear an utterance from His mouth. For you will be a witness for Him to all men of what you have seen and heard."

—Acts 22:12–15

Paul was empowered with four distinct privileges that exemplified his apostolic calling.

1. Appointed to know His will
2. To see the Righteous One
3. To hear utterances from His lips
4. To be a witness, or testifier, of what was seen and heard

Witness is a judicial term signifying someone testifying of what one has personally seen and heard. Hearsay evidence is disallowed in a court proceeding. Anointed eyes and ears are essential to accomplish this mandate by granting access to Heaven's revelatory realm. By the Spirit of Revelation we apprehend God's will and articulate as credible witnesses the testimony of spiritual truth we have seen and heard.

Paul functioned as an overseer in God's storehouse and ministered as a steward at the time of the Pentecost harvest. Likewise, in the in-gathering harvest, many overseers will be empowered with genuine spiritual authority to bring in the great harvest. These artisans will work within cities and regions that function as storehouses.

A present work of the Spirit is to initiate the process of gathering the stumbling blocks and obstacles set against God's highest purposes. As we petition Heaven to release the "ministering spirits who gather" through our delegated authority, we will watch these elements extracted and a more abundant flow of grace supplied to initiate genuine governmental leadership.

We have the incredible opportunity to have spiritual stumbling blocks extracted through the administration of this word. Many intercessory prayer ministries have been seeking a strategy—here is an end-time blueprint. Prayer movements can empower the "angels that gather" to fulfill the outline of the Matthew 13 parable.

TWO HARVESTS

We are being called to two predominant harvests. Following the Lord's ministry 120 believers were set apart, prepared, and then unleashed to transform their generation. First, the Lord harvested 120 radical followers who tarried for a season until the appropriate time for their release. When the Day of Pentecost had fully come the floodgate was opened and they were loosed to change the world.

Much the same pattern is being established today. Initially a body of people who have been pruned and refined will be harvested and set apart to await their release. They will be gathered into the storehouses by overseers exerting spiritual authority over realms of darkness to collect them. When the appropriate time comes, they will be commissioned to transform the twenty-first century.

The world is going to become exceedingly dark. When believers are the only bearers of light and life, the principles of Genesis 41 will become reality. Egypt was the only nation with a storehouse of wheat and became the most powerful nation on the face of the earth at that time because of this divine strategy. When the Church becomes filled with life and light as darkness covers the earth, people will stream to our light.

This current outpouring will produce a harvest of harvesters, awaiting the day of famine, as wheat was stored in the barns of Egypt anticipating the lean years to come.

However, they will not be dormant—quite the contrary. This ingathering will harvest people from diverse backgrounds and spiritual conditions, safeguarding and preparing them through accelerated programs and schools to await their release. Great activity and equipping will be operating, as with Paul in his period of readiness and revelation in the Arabian

Desert, until the appointed time when he was dispatched into his apostolic charge.

Our Joseph, the Lord Jesus Christ, is being commissioned by His Father to implement the plan outlined in this passage. All authority in Heaven and in earth has been given to Him for its accomplishment. He is searching for overseers to whom He can impart this governmental mandate with heavenly authority to bring in one in five.

He is looking for people who possess the character and nature of trustworthy stewards so that He can appoint and commission them. This principle is directly related to the functions of the Tabernacle of David. David's Tabernacle functioned in prayer, praise, and prophetic proclamations. However, a specific strategy needs to be applied to these functions. This Joseph blueprint shows us one of those strategies.

Men and women functioning in this overseer anointing will be delegates of Heaven's authority, declaring into the spiritual realm a calling in of one in five. When they do, "angels that gather" will be empowered to scour the surrounding region and collect into the storehouses a company of people who will be gathered and guarded until the appointed time.

The New Ministry Model

Growth demands change, and change warrants growth! Two attributes will clearly identify the coming years—transformation and maturation. Both will characterize a body of people who introduce a new ministry model to the twenty-first century Church.

The prophetic platforms mentioned in the previous chapter utilized to glean a measure of harvest may be somewhat different from those of the past. Delegated spiritual authority to overseers, storehouses for a place of refuge and equipping, and angels working with us to gather the harvest are all principles of God's Kingdom we will come to know much more fluently. They represent symbolic pictures of how many individuals, churches, and ministries are being prepared to steward powerful Heavenly endowments.

Though they may seem fresh and unprecedented, these precepts are actually a reintroduction of godly standards that are both relevant and biblically based.

As Solomon emphasized in Ecclesiastes:

> I know that everything God does will remain forever;
> there is nothing to add to it and there is nothing to
> take from it, for God has so worked that men should
> fear Him. That which is has been already and that
> which will be has already been, for God seeks what has
> passed by.
>
> —Ecclesiastes 3:14–15

Many in the twenty-first century Church world are discovering that religious activity does not equate to Christ-likeness. Everything that can be shaken is being tried to the core, and the fallout is sometimes devastating. Nevertheless, God's Kingdom marches on, and His plan progressively unfolds to an awaiting generation.

Certainly there has been no lack of effort and human energy applied toward various programs, models, and strategies for the promised harvest. Obviously, most people giving themselves unstintingly to these programs are sincere and seek the Lord's pleasure. Nevertheless, the Bible is plain: Sincerity alone is insufficient—it must be merged with truth.

Cain's sincerity equaled Abel's, but his sacrifice was rejected. Although he spent countless hours working the fields, pruning the crops, and gathering the harvest, his tithe from the fruit of the ground was refused because it wasn't merged with revelation and didn't follow God's pattern.

Likewise, though Martha was sincere and diligent in her duties, Mary was the one commended for desiring a more excellent way. Perhaps all of us have experienced this quandary at some point. We are currently being afforded a profound opportunity to realign ourselves with Heaven and appropriate our resources and energy in partnership with the Holy Spirit. That is the entering His rest spoken of in the book of Hebrews. The Lord is ardently looking for those who will rest in Him so He can rest in them.

FINDING HIS REST

Three Hebrew sons were thrust into Nebuchadnezzar's fiery furnace; but they trusted God to save them, even if their physical bodies perished in flames. Their extraordinary faith aroused God's affections. He did not let them face this crisis alone; He entered the trial with them so they could discover His rest. Not even the smell of smoke was allowed to touch these devoted men. They had entered God's rest.

Spiritual rest is an essential element that must be ascertained in its fullness in order to overcome the fear and terror that will permeate this generation. We are living in a time of extremes. The hearts of those who are not grounded in Christ will be inundated with intense fear and intimidation. Conversely, extravagant faith, trust, and rest will be delegated to those fully submitted to the Lord and His perfect plan.

Grace is being released to facilitate comprehension and personal apprehension of this dimension of the faith realm. When we articulate this desire to the Father through prayer, praise, and prophetic proclamations, a spiritual dynamic is unleashed that produces this supernatural arena. That truth represents a portion of the new ministry model on the horizon, as Isaiah declared:

> You have heard [these things foretold], now you see
> this fulfillment. And will you not bear witness to it?
> I show you specified new things from this time forth,
> even hidden things [kept in reserve] which you have
> not known. They are created now [called into being
> by the prophetic word], and not long ago; and before
> today you have never heard of them, lest you should
> say, Behold, I knew them!
> —Isaiah 48:6–7, AMP

These "new things" will have as much impact on the twenty-first century Church as the Azusa Street Revival did in the twentieth century. Throughout Church history diverse expressions of God's Spirit have been released in the earth, with each deposit increasingly conveying His attributes and a further understanding of His ways. Ultimately, each was intended to reveal the Lord Jesus Christ and His Kingdom.

Since the days of Martin Luther, our biblical heritage has been progressively restored. The end-time will be marked as a season of revealing and restoring truth, while also exposing the hidden devices of darkness that have deceived the people of the earth.

We stand on the brink of another exceptional unveiling of God's plan for humanity. It will launch one of the greatest demonstrations of His Kingdom ever experienced, as well as reformulate a new and more complete understanding of the Lord and the full measure of His redemptive plan.

The Lord is establishing a foundation of righteousness on the earth upon which He will allow the authority of His throne to rest. Once fashioned, it cannot be moved from its place. What He is setting in motion will continue without end. The time has now arrived for the fullness of the revelation of Christ to be delegated to a prophesied and foreknown generation.

MOBILIZATION OF THE BODY

We do not know exactly what the next outpouring of God's Spirit will look like, but we do know it will require the mobilization of the Body of Christ. Not only will leadership need to enter into this place of intimate fellowship with God, but also all of His people. Paul saw this unity as a platform for spiritual impartation, attesting:

> For I long to see you so that I may impart some
> spiritual gift to you, that you may be established; that
> is, that I may be encouraged together with you while

among you, each of us by the other's faith, both yours
and mine.

—Romans 1:11–12

Paul desired to impart a spiritual deposit to the people; and he
engaged a Kingdom principle to achieve this objective. He aspired
to be strengthened and encouraged, along with the Church, by the
cooperation of their faith.

He saw the alliance of his faith with that of the Roman
believers as a conduit to blessings. The consolidation of faith
between spiritual leaders and God's people will touch Heaven
and transform the spiritual atmosphere of this world. It will
revolutionize the spiritual climate of a region.

An awakening is brewing; a fresh, new breath on the horizon.
The mandate being placed upon the twenty-first century Church,
when accessed, will in its effects be as impacting as the last
century's 1906 outpouring.

The Holy Spirit's presence that enabled Paul's and John's
ministries is with us too. Our prayer should now be, as was theirs,
for the merger of leadership's faith with God's people's to release
the spiritual impartation necessary to birth this next season.
Believers' faith in cooperation with apostolic leaders can access
God's throne and open the windows of Heaven in a city or region.
A spiritual transference then manifests that impacts individuals,
churches, cities, and nations.

The energizing of our consolidated faith with the Spirit's
supernatural anointing is the way of God's Kingdom and a
portion of the "new thing" being established. It functions best
when we apprehend God's plan and desire through revelatory
insight, before consolidating it with our faith to change a region's
spiritual climate.

We must always remember that victory will not be achieved
because of any virtue of our own, but rather because of His

goodness and His commitment to Heaven's biblical plan for this age. His loving-kindness and grace is the force releasing the revelation of Kingdom power and authority in the earth. We have only the prerogative to touch Heaven and bring its reality to the earth, as Jesus prayed, "Your kingdom come. Your will be done on earth as it is in heaven."

A prophetic allotment of revelatory truth from His Word will be achieved in this generation; hidden manna, reserved for the last-days' generation, accessed and anointed to mobilize His people. Although much will not be realized in fullness until Jesus returns, great and profound realities await achievement before His second coming. The bride He will return to is without spot or wrinkle; a bride who lives abundantly and victoriously as those who overcome the spirit of this world.

GROUNDING THE UNPRECEDENTED

The previously unknown events that took place in the first century were grounded in the prophetic outline detailed in the Old Testament Scriptures. The spiritual phenomena were so fresh and unprecedented, the Spirit of Revelation had to highlight and illumine the ancient prophets' utterances in order for them to be fully understood.

Pentecost had no precedent. A revelatory anointing was essential to rightly divide the Word of Truth and match their experience to God's Word. Peter preached that:

> These are not drunken, as ye suppose, seeing it is but
> the third hour of the day. But this is that which was
> spoken by the prophet Joel...
> —Acts 2:15–16, KJV

Peter confirmed, "This is that which was spoken by the prophet Joel," and thereby established for all future generations a model for understanding historic prophecies under a new covenant application. Previously veiled and mystical passages were being fulfilled in their midst, as they shall continue to be. The revelatory anointing is necessary to fully comprehend God's purposes as well as biblically settle their validity.

The Pentecost outpouring had a firstruits harvest associated with it. The Feast of Firstfruits foreshadowed much of what the book of Acts and the early apostolic age demonstrated. God used ordinary people who received an extraordinary mandate and Heaven's virtue to achieve its fulfillment. The lives and characteristics of the first century disciples exhibit a clear standard to qualify for God's army. All experienced personal failure and were seemingly void of the traits considered requisite in world changing leaders; yet, God used them profoundly, and He will use us as well...if we meet Him on His terms.

Paul announced that he had not forsaken his responsibility to inform his generation of the whole council of God. As shepherd, overseer, and commissioned officer, he was charged and empowered with Kingdom authority to scout the fields of humanity and reap a firstfruits harvest to fulfill the prophetic significance of the early feasts. Miracles, signs, and wonders authenticated men and women with apostolic and governmental authority to achieve this harvest.

In ancient Israel the initial harvest was the "firstfruits" harvest and the second, more predominant one was the "ingathering." Pentecost (*Shavuot*) typifies firstfruits harvest while the Feast of Tabernacles (*Sukkot*) is a model of the ingathering harvest. The prophetic outline the Lord utilized in firstfruits also offers important understanding about the ingathering.

The Lord is raising up a governmental people endowed with His Kingdom's authority who will go into the fields of humanity to draw the harvest to Himself. He shall receive the full measure of His reward for his sufferings.

TABERNACLE OF DAVID ADMINISTRATION

The prophet Amos prophesied regarding two incredible aspects of the end-time mandate. He predicted that the Jewish people would be restored out of the Diaspora to their Promised Land. Never before in human history had a nation been totally dismantled, with their government, economy, and language completely eradicated, then fully restored after twenty-five hundred years. That unprecedented event happened when the Jewish homeland of Israel was recognized as a nation in 1948.

Amos also prophesied that the Tabernacle of David would be restored, foretelling:

> "On that day I will raise up
> The tabernacle of David, which has fallen down,
> And repair its damages;
> I will raise up its ruins,
> And rebuild it as in the days of old."
>
> —Amos 9:11, NKJV

An exceedingly interesting phenomenon occurred in the early Church—one the Jewish believers of the day had not anticipated—Gentiles received the good news of Jesus Christ and were filled with the Holy Spirit. The first century apostolic leaders were then confronted with reconciling their theology to this actuality and the prophetic Scriptures with this unforeseen blessing. Concurrently, James received the following word of wisdom from the Holy Spirit, direct from God's heart:

> Simon has declared how God at the first visited the
> Gentiles to take out of them a people for His name.
> And with this the words of the prophets agree, just as it
> is written:

"After this I will return
And will rebuild the tabernacle of David, which has fallen
  down;
I will rebuild its ruins,
And I will set it up;
So that the rest of mankind may seek the LORD,
Even all the Gentiles who are called by My name,
Says the LORD who does all these things."

Known to God from eternity are all His works.
                             —Acts 15:14–18, NKJV

James directly applied Amos' well-known prophetic promise to the Gentile dispensation. The Lord also foretold His plan to re-gather a people dispersed across the nations of the earth, upon whom He would assign His name. Both applications of Amos' prophecy are being fulfilled in this generation. As certain as Israel has now been restored to her homeland, so also will the Tabernacle of David be reestablished to her full administration!

Many of the Lord's Jewish brethren did not recognize Him at His first appearing; therefore, He is securing for Himself a predominantly Gentile bride who will be sent away when the time comes to reveal Himself to Israel at His second coming.

The Tabernacle of David administration is progressing and maturing in relationship to our end-time mandate. This prophetic model is a bridal paradigm that will play a pivotal role in the harvest; not just for worshipers, but the entirety of God's bride.

Through prayer, praise, and prophetic decrees issued through Tabernacle of David restoration, an angelic host will be empowered to co-labor with us to bring in a harvest of laborers. Heaven's host will surround this generation and fulfill David's psalm of blessing:

Bless the LORD, you His angels,
Mighty in strength, who perform His word,
Obeying the voice of His word!

—Psalm 103:20

The same administration will help equip and prepare the harvesters for the great harvest. This generation will invoke living expressions of the Lord and His Kingdom through a people set apart for such a destiny. They will set in motion this prophetic strategy to harvest from this generation's "wheat" fields a bridal company who will be empowered with the Lord's virtue to fulfill His end-of-time mandates.

Many "harp and bowl" gatherings are seeking prophetic strategy by engaging the revelatory realm to apprehend Heaven's blueprint for this generation. The "angels that gather" message is an aspect of that strategy. Insightful prayer, heartfelt worship, and laser like prophetic proclamations empower Heaven's host, while faith filled recitals of Scripture authorize angels to fulfill God's plan on earth. This Kingdom principle is designed to reward the Savior in full measure for His sacrifice on our behalf.

DECREES AND PROCLAMATIONS
On the morning of December 24, 2004, I awakened from a dream and heard the Scriptures quoted directly.

For I am the LORD your God, who stirs up the sea
and its waves roar (the LORD of hosts is His name). "I
have put My words in your mouth and have covered
you with the shadow of My hand, to establish the
heavens, to found the earth, and to say to Zion, 'You
are My people.'"

—Isaiah 51:15–16

Living in Orange Beach, Alabama, this passage immediately proved meaningful to me, for just three months before, on September 16, Hurricane Ivan had devastated our hometown with a twenty-five-foot wall of water. Full recovery would take years.

Even so, this strategic Scripture had even greater meaning two days later, when on December 26, 2004, another event caused me to view the fifteenth verse from an entirely new perspective. On this date the tragic Asian tsunami took place, in which the seas truly were stirred and the waves roared in an unprecedented way.

I hadn't forecasted the Asian tsunami from this experience, but the event's magnitude definitively affirms to me the truth resident in the sixteenth verse is a present word.

END-TIME IMPARTATION

The Lord has often utilized this passage through prophetic experiences to illustrate a function of His end-time army. The Bible promises that He will put a prophetic word in our mouths replete with life and power; a word issuing directly from His heart and establishing this Kingdom revelation.

Furthermore, it is critical that when this impartation manifests it be pronounced from an atmosphere of spiritual anointing.

"I have put My words in your mouth and have covered you with the shadow of My hand..." The overshadowing of His hand is the forum from which decrees and proclamations must proceed. Mary was overshadowed by the power of the Most High and her agreement with Him was creative. This is an illustration of His anointing for power and authority. Such cooperation between Word and Spirit will not fail but will accomplish every purpose for which it is intended.

When the Lord puts His Word in our mouths and covers us with the shadow of His hand, the resulting prophetic directive is meant to accomplish three things:

1. Establish the heavens
2. Found the earth
3. Say to Zion, "You are My people."

Angels commissioned as divine winds serve to carry and escalate the fiery words proceeding from the mouths of the Lord's messengers. Throughout the Lord's ministry angelic activity abounded. Likewise, substantial angelic activity will accompany today's ministers of the Lord to help orchestrate the divine visitation promised to this generation and to position them to receive it.

People will be greatly surprised to discover the far-reaching effects their words have as the angels bear anointed messages to the far corners of the earth. The word of the Lord proceeding from anointed vessels will be transported and carried by the winds of these angels to strategic individuals and regions with transformative impact.

ON EARTH AS IN HEAVEN

Jeremiah was privileged to have an incredible face-to-face encounter with the Lord. He described it thus:

> Then the LORD stretched out His hand and touched my
> mouth, and the LORD said to me, "Behold, I have put
> My words in your mouth. See, I have appointed you this
> day over the nations and over the kingdoms,
>
> To pluck up and to break down,
> To destroy and to overthrow,
> To build and to plant."
> —Jeremiah 1:9–10

God's Spirit is delegating Kingdom authority today to

accomplish the same commission Jeremiah received. We are being appointed with spiritual oversight to root out, pull down, destroy, and overthrow, but also to build and plant. That is also the directive of Isaiah 51:16.

What is established in the heavenly places will be released on earth. When this comes to pass the bridal company will be called out to assume her rightful place of power and authority for the great harvest. The Holy Spirit is addressing the seeds of destiny resident in the Zion Company avowing, "You are My people." We will be identified as bone of His bone and flesh of His flesh to accomplish the same mandate Jesus was given by His Father—to announce the redemption message and destroy the devil's works (1 John 3:8).

The spiritual atmosphere surrounding a region dictates that territory's characteristics. For instance, if spirits of witchcraft and sorcery predominantly occupy the heavenly places over a region, then many people living under that jurisdiction will be captured by these spirits. Conversely, if an open Heaven prevails over a territory, then righteousness and truth will flourish, many souls will be harvested, and God's people will abide in divine fellowship and fruitfulness.

Testimonies concerning South American cities that experienced transformation provide evidence of this reality. Territories previously bound by corruption became totally renewed spiritually and naturally, inducing even the vegetation to respond to God's Kingdom revelation with unparalleled produce yields.

OUR MANDATE

Many Christians are being positioned to experience this commissioning. The Lord is stretching forth His hand to fill our mouths with decrees and proclamations direct from His heart. As with Jeremiah, the anointed words of God's people will uproot the forces of darkness and plant Kingdom revelation to beckon His sons and daughters to maturity.

When the moment of Israel's liberation from Egypt arrived, the enemy was impotent to prohibit God's decree. Heavenly decrees issued forth through angelic "watchers" bear God's authority. Not even the Red Sea could prevent the accomplishment of that decree. Pharaoh's army was annihilated under the weight of this command.

So is it today! We are living in a day of restoration. The fortunes of God's inheritance are being replenished. Great will be the rejoicing of those ascending Mount Zion to experience the awesome spiritual blessings ordained for this day.

Our song will be:

"Worthy are You to take the book and to break its
seals; for You were slain, and purchased for God with
Your blood men from every tribe and tongue and
people and nation."
                                              —Revelation 5:9

Then from our innermost being will flow springs of living water to quench the thirst of a parched land. We are the rock through which the water will flow; He is the source, we the vessels He uses. Many will be "sent" to dry and desolate places as a source of life through which springs of Heavenly water will flow.

The Scripture plainly asserts—the Lord ever lives to make intercession on our behalf (Hebrews 7:25). If there was ever a time to draw near to God to apprehend His heart and desire, it is now, in this generation. The Lord is continually beseeching His bride to join with His intercessory heart for this prophetic generation. When we do, our prophetic decrees will be more accurate because the Lord's heart will have generated them.

Springs of living water will proceed from the mouths of the Lord's messengers with evangelistic power that will quench the thirst of the lost and desperate. Greater evangelism will sprout outside church walls, as an army of Kingdom missionaries will be anointed and sent to difficult and oppressive areas with Heaven's commission to provide living water.

We now live in a season of spiritual breakthrough. A heavenly host has been dispatched; our responsibility is to articulate the Lord's desire through an anointed atmosphere building Kingdom revelation. The battle is won in the Spirit first then manifested in the natural. This is our strategy for corporate breakthrough in this portion of God's plan.

DAWNING OF A NEW DAY

A new day is dawning both for those in and outside Christ. It is a new day of light and in the realms of darkness.

> For in the day of trouble He will conceal me in His
>   tabernacle;
> In the secret place of His tent He will hide me;
> He will lift me up on a rock.
>
> And now my head will be lifted up above my
>   enemies around me,
> And I will offer in His tent sacrifices with shouts
>   of joy;
> I will sing, yes, I will sing praises to the Lord.
>
> —Psalm 27:5–6

There will be times and seasons to hide ourselves in Christ and other times to be aggressive and militant in our posture. When we spend time isolated with Him, we are not dormant; instead, we are waiting and ministering to Him to glean His insight and blueprint for victory.

O LORD, I love the habitation of Your house
And the place where Your glory dwells.
Do not take my soul away along with sinners,
Nor my life with men of bloodshed,
In whose hands is a wicked scheme,
And whose right hand is full of bribes.
—Psalm 26:8–10

When we wait upon the Lord we will mount up with a revelatory anointing expressed through an eagle's attributes, which grants further understanding of His scheme for triumph. We can then rally the troops behind that directive in much the same way David became the victorious king in his battles with Israel's enemies.

WINDS IN THE MULBERRY TREE

God's winds are once again blowing in the mulberry trees on behalf of the righteous. This notable statement indicates a supernatural release of heavenly virtue on behalf of God's saints for breakthrough and quick advance.

"And it shall be, when you hear the sound of marching
in the tops of the mulberry trees, then you shall
advance quickly. For then the LORD will go out before
you to strike the camp of the Philistines." And David
did so, as the LORD commanded him; and he drove
back the Philistines from Geba as far as Gezer.
—2 Samuel 5:24–25

This spiritual application is true on multiple levels. Miracles, signs, and wonders will palpably accompany the Lord's people in pronounced ways along with a substantial increase in the healing anointing. This time will mark the beginning of a season of favor that will escalate until the end of the age. When we hear the "new" sound of marching in the mulberry trees, we will know the Lord is with us for advancement.

This promise is heightened for those who have embraced this commission by yielding themselves to the grooming and preparatory process. Yielded vessels wholly submitted to Him derive righteousness through the release of divine grace. Righteousness and justice are His throne's foundation. To experience the governmental release of Kingdom dominion, we must also allow the Holy Spirit to equip us as overcomers clothed in garments of righteousness.

CHAPTER

4

The

Transition

"My people are destroyed for lack of knowledge!" (Hosea 4:6). What an alarming statement by the Lord's prophet concerning His people. Hosea was addressing the moral corruption and spiritual adultery permeating his generation. Despite outwardly experiencing a time of notable prosperity and growth, Israel was deteriorating in their relationship with the Lord.

We reside in the information age, where access to historical data, Christian teachings, and general information has never been so accessible or abundant. Still, despite the copious resources at our disposal, a significant percentage of Christians remain comparatively uninformed of our rich heritage and the meticulous unfolding of God's plan throughout the last century. Many destinies are perishing without fulfillment because of a lack of understanding of the times, regardless of the wealth of information and finances available. Nevertheless, a great awakening is at hand.

The Reformation initiated an era of progressive recovery of Bible truth and the refurbishment of various ministries lost during the Dark Ages. Careful examination shows that each spiritual outpouring has highlighted unique qualities of God's character and our redemptive birthrights. The Holy Spirit has now ushered us in to a pivotal point in history necessitating fresh revelations from His heart. Revelatory truth will mobilize and equip an army of believers to meet the resounding demands of a lost and misguided generation.

A harvest is ripening! We must aggressively prepare to receive them into the storehouses for accelerated training and grooming. In the same way Azusa Street transformed twentieth century Christianity, this unveiling of God's plan will revolutionize the twenty-first century perception of Christian faith.

In large proportion this will be achieved by ministries functioning as havens of spiritual rest, and as "schools of the spirit." Something of great spiritual value is being imparted to us to help God's emerging leaders qualify in Spirit and truth.

THE ORIGINAL MODEL

The early Church ministry was profound on many levels. By natural standards, its leader's credentials were singularly unimpressive. Generally, their personal abilities failed to qualify them for their pioneering assignments. Regardless, they received divine impartation to validate their mission and facilitate God's Kingdom revelation. They believed God and trusted not in their own strength but in His.

The Bible plainly recounts the various signs and awesome healing power accompanying the early Church in their task. Scripture informs us that reverential awe fell upon many as miraculous wonders took place. As a result people were added to the Church daily, and God's name was notably glorified.

We need these same results today. Our assignment is no less important or difficult than the early apostolic Church's; in fact, in various ways ours is even more complex and involved. Therefore, we need all the empowerment they had and multiplied.

The early disciples preached the Gospel of the Kingdom and ministered to people's spirit, soul, and body. They did not "shrink from declaring the whole purpose of God." Furthermore, in the midst of persecution and an unbelieving generation, their message was confirmed through the Holy Spirit's power imparted to them at Pentecost. They prayed for confirmation of His Word saying:

> ...grant to Your servants that with all boldness they may speak Your word, by stretching out Your hand to heal, and that signs and wonders may be done through the name of Your holy Servant Jesus.
> —Acts 4:29–30, NKJV

Divine power testifies of the gospel. That is why the first believers passionately prayed for empowerment with signs and wonders as a means of conveying the good news of the Kingdom and winning the lost.

A MORE SURE WORD

Never has the need been more desperate for a clear prophetic word direct from God's heart. The Lord told me prophetically that our introduction into the twenty-first century would mark times of transition and change. As the saying goes, "Life is pleasant. Death is peaceful. It's the transition that's troublesome."

Transition is defined as "the act of passing from one state or place into the next." Change is "the result of an alteration or modification." The transitions of recent years initiated a process that will usher in great change. Our response and willingness to align with Heaven's plans will determine our fruitfulness.

Genuine spiritual change is only wrought by divine visitation. The Reformation was incited by a prophetic declaration from God's heart. A fullness-of-time moment had occurred in God's plan and the ministry of restoration was set in motion. That movement has been progressively accelerating to this present hour. Another crossroad has been met and great change is imminent.

With a fresh word from the Lord arises an equally important need for augmentation and honing of discernment. History attests that a deluge of voices has accompanied each major juncture in God's timeline. Notwithstanding, the Lord promised that His sheep would know His voice.

> "When he puts forth all his own, he goes ahead of them,
> and the sheep follow him because they know his voice.
> A stranger they simply will not follow, but will flee from
> him, because they do not know the voice of strangers."
> —John 10:4–5

When we discern His voice, however, it must evoke an affirmative response or we will be doomed to repeat past mistakes. Since Israel's exodus from Egypt, a consistent pattern has developed following each visitation of God's Spirit. Biblical and natural history exhibits that without revelatory insight, we will miss the day of our visitation. Moses rebuked his generation maintaining:

> ..."You have seen all that the LORD did before your eyes
> in the land of Egypt to Pharaoh and all his servants and
> all his land; the great trials which your eyes have seen,
> those great signs and wonders. Yet to this day the LORD
> has not given you a heart to know, nor eyes to see, nor
> ears to hear..."
> —Deuteronomy 29:2–4

For forty years the Lord daily performed miracles on behalf of a nation devoid of revelatory understanding of their real purpose. As a result, Israel missed their invitation to enter the promise, and Moses disqualified himself because of frustration with the people's lack of comprehension.

Isaiah was commissioned to prophesy to a people also lacking eyes to see, ears to hear, and a heart to understand the Kingdom message. That generation also missed their day of visitation. They did not comprehend the message nor did they receive God's messenger. The Apocrypha tells us that Isaiah was "sawn asunder with a wooden saw" because of that generation's hardness of heart and absence of revelatory insight.

History clearly demonstrates that without the Spirit of Revelation, God's people will reject the heavenly invitation and martyr the messengers who bring it. As the apostle John highlighted, this was true even with the promised Messiah. Despite the most incredible miracle ministry in history, the people would still not believe. John reported:

> Though He had performed so many signs before them,
> yet they were not believing in Him; This was to fulfill
> the word of Isaiah the prophet which he spoke, "LORD,
> WHO HAS BELIEVED OUR REPORT? AND TO WHOM
> HAS THE ARM OF THE LORD BEEN REVEALED?"
>
> For this reason they could not believe, for Isaiah
> said again, "HE HAS BLINDED THEIR EYES,
> AND HE HARDENED THEIR HEART; SO THAT
> THEY WOULD NOT SEE WITH THEIR EYES,
> AND PERCEIVE WITH THEIR HEART, AND BE
> CONVERTED, AND I HEAL THEM."
> —John 12:37-40

The end result was only 120 who faithfully embraced the message among the generation that crucified the Messiah.

APPREHENDING THE MESSSAGE

The Gospel of the Kingdom is the power of God leading to salvation. This gospel does not merely consist in words but also in God's sovereign power. The ministry of signs and wonders does not diminish the supernatural nature of God's written Word—it merely confirms it.

The Lord demonstrates His power through miracles, signs, and wonders and authenticates a message that is firmly rooted and grounded in the written Word. God's people are often captivated by signs and wonders, but only a remnant is captured by the message. This trend must be reversed. The early Church model stipulated:

> And they went out and preached everywhere, while the Lord worked with them, and confirmed the word by the signs that followed.
>
> —Mark 16:20

God's revealed Word is incontrovertibly established by the Holy Spirit's endorsement, consisting of approval or affirmation exhibited through signs, wonders, and manifestations of the Spirit. The Holy Spirit punctuated the early disciple's labor with the miraculous to confirm God's Kingdom message. Supernatural confirmation functioned as a divine validation, sealing messages firmly grounded in the written Word, but with fresh applications. Historically, we have been so disproportionately fascinated with miracle working power that we have allowed it to overshadow the importance of the message.

Spiritual grace is being allotted to quicken the spirits of this generation to receive His present-day manna. A supernatural hunger is provoking us to move beyond cold, formal religiosity to pursue intimate relationship with Him. To even possess this desire is God's gift. We simply do not retain the ability within ourselves to carry out God's ultimate plan.

We need God and the embodiment of His Spirit to fuel us with power. For, as wonderful and necessary as magnificent displays of the Spirit are, the quest to know Him as the Living Word remains our most vital calling. Ministries desperately need the validation of His power, but we cannot allow that to become the end in itself. It is only a means to the end—union with the Lord is our ultimate destiny.

A TWENTIETH CENTURY TOKEN

In each expression of spiritual outpouring throughout church history, God's presence was authenticated with various manifestations of His Spirit. During the early twentieth century, Maria Woodworth-Etter's ministry prompted amazing spiritual signs and miraculous wonders like the early apostolic believers.

The Bible promised to "bear witness" to the Kingdom message with diverse miracles and gifts of the Holy Spirit (Hebrews 2:4). This truth was not limited to the early Church, but is available in every age for those willing to press into God for its release. The marvelous displays of healing and deliverance prevalent in Woodworth-Etter's meetings were similar to that generated on behalf of the first century believers. Many people tended to "fall under the power" in her services and remain in that condition for days.

Doctors would often examine those in this condition to ascertain their heart rate and other vital signs. In each case the individual was determined to be in a perfectly healthy state. They were taken by God's Spirit and struck prostrate without food, water, or movement. Some remained in this condition as long as seven days; facts confirmed by both the secular and Christian medias.

Tremendous testimonies of healing, deliverance, and divine commissions were well documented to accompany these encounters. While experiencing these signs and wonders, many were commissioned to foreign lands and emerged able to fluently speak the language of the nation to which they were commissioned. Various accounts reported that the spirit of conviction attending these manifestations was so deep as to melt the most hardened characters into weeping repentance.

This depicts a token of the heritage God desires for His people and the empowerment of His presence essential to the fulfillment of our latter-day mandate.

PURSUIT OF MATURITY

As previously mentioned, "change demands growth, and growth warrants change." A legitimate and experiential encounter with the Living Word will kindle a fruitful and needed change. The Spirit's revelatory anointing illumines our spiritual eyes and ears to grant access to His thoughts and ways. When we learn to maneuver according to His ways, notable advancement is the final outcome. Intense changes will ensue when the Bride of Christ grows out of adolescence into maturity, which this juncture of Church history will exhibit. The writer of Hebrews asserted:

> For though by this time you ought to be teachers,
> you have need again for someone to teach you the
> elementary principles of the oracles of God, and
> you have come to need milk and not solid food. For
> everyone who partakes only of milk is not accustomed
> to the word of righteousness, for he is an infant. But
> solid food is for the mature, who because of practice
> have their senses trained to discern good and evil.
> —Hebrews 5:12–14

A contention is presently raging in heavenly places, and God desires that we appropriate the spiritual high ground. I was taught how important godly maturity is to facilitate this process by a revelation in which I was shown a young boy constantly taunted by a schoolyard bully. Year after year this overbearing bully would torment the young lad, take his lunch money, and generally make life miserable. As the experience continued, the young lad grew into a mature young man who developed physically and emotionally.

After a period of absence the bully surfaced once again expecting to resume his persecution as before. However, the young man was different now; he had grown up. And what had previously been a source of great fear and intimidation, now seemed trivial and merely a passing nuisance for the young man. The bully had not changed; only the young man had progressed into maturity.

GROWING UP

This analogy depicts our present call. What seemed menacing and domineering previously proves menial in spiritual adulthood. The Holy Spirit often allows the existence of spiritual "bullies" to train us in maturity and spark us to grow up. Joseph's betrayal and dungeon experience was necessary to geographically relocate him to his place of destiny, and it also conditioned him to rule.

In spiritual adolescence our attempts to rise above the ashes of defeat to fulfill a heavenly mandate seem to be often met by the thief, rushing in like a flood to drown our calling. But once we grow into our divine legacy as "sons of the Kingdom," enemies who previously succeeded in stealing our inheritance will no longer be fruitful. Throughout this present age, fear of man and spirits of intimidation will be extracted by believers living this reality. Like the prophetic word given to Job, "Though your beginning was insignificant, Yet your end will increase greatly" (Job 8:7).

This transition from adolescence to maturity will cause the Church's mind-set to shift into a more militant, warlike attitude. Circumstances previously appearing fearsome and insurmountable will suddenly seem trivial as we progress into Christ-likeness and press into spiritual maturity. Such will be the heritage of those who overcome and act as the "Joshuas" of the twenty-first century.

A major emphasis throughout the Church ages has been to produce mature believers who discover the secret to overcoming the spirit of this world. Our ultimate call is to rule and reign with Him as joint heirs. We will recognize the mark of the end of the age by the maturing of both seeds of light and darkness and the reaping of good and evil. Spiritual maturity is mandatory in this conflict, along with a thorough understanding of our present place in Church history and God's prophetic time line.

Many hearts have been prepared to encounter the Lord. Tremendous revelatory truth promised in God's Word will be released in this exchange. The prophet Daniel was given panoramic visions of this time but was not permitted to relinquish the revelation. It was reserved for this specific moment in human history. That certainty alone ought to prompt us to rise above the spirit of this world to apprehend our individual destiny.

GOD'S ABSOLUTE

Paul is another prophetic leadership model to emulate today. His gospel came neither by human education nor by the reading of a book, but rather by divine revelation (Galatians 1:12). His message was an absolute standard with heavenly authentication.

The same level of revelation granted to Paul is about to be released to inform the Church of God's "plumb line," which will serve to establish a perfect standard. Our comprehension of God's Word will rocket to incredible heights when we eat the now "open book" of redemption unveiling the fullness of God's plan. John was representing a bridal company when he was commanded to:

> ..."Go, take the book which is open in the hand of the
> angel who stands on the sea and on the land...Take it
> and eat it; it will make your stomach bitter, but in your

mouth it will be sweet as honey...You must prophesy again concerning many peoples and nations and tongues and kings."

—Revelation 10:8–11

These revelations have been reserved in God from Daniel's day until today. The treasures of wisdom and knowledge hidden in Christ that will render the Bride of Christ without spot or wrinkle will be delegated to her.

There has been something woven into the spiritual DNA of God's people that propel us into this new place; a place of "deep calling unto deep." And God will respond to our desperation by releasing from His throne the Voice of the seven thunders promised in Revelation 10.

God's Kingdom mysteries are poised to be set in motion to awaken and equip the Bride of Christ. That is our current purpose and our quest. Our purest counsel to participate in this plan is to respond to the wooing of God's Spirit. Divine mobilization will prompt us to lay aside every weight and encumbrance that has previously entangled us. So, today, if we hear His Voice, we cannot harden our hearts to this fresh message. According to the Psalmist:

> For He is our God,
> And we are the people of His pasture and the sheep
>   of His hand.
> Today, if you would hear His voice,
> Do not harden your hearts, as at Meribah,
> As in the day of Massah in the wilderness...
>
> —Psalm 95:7–8

The Lord has been restraining spiritual issues to allow preparation, both spiritually and naturally. Likewise, our enemy has attempted to escalate things before their time. This has been the contention experienced by many saints in this generation.

A FIRSTFRUITS HARVEST

A firstfruits harvest is maturing so that God's plan can be set in motion. This company of men and women will be gathered into the storehouses created by the Holy Spirit to be trained, equipped, and entrusted with the virtues of overcomers.

VIRTUES OF THE OVERCOMER

1. To eat from the tree of life which is in the midst of the Paradise of God (Revelation 2:7)
2. Protection from the second death (Revelation 2:11)
3. To eat of the hidden manna and receive a white stone with a new name written upon it (Revelation 2:17)
4. Authority over the nations and the bright morning star (Revelation 2:27–28)
5. To be clothed in white garments and our name confessed before the Father and His angels (Revelation 3:5)
6. To be a pillar in the temple of God and the name of our God and of His city, the New Jerusalem written on them. (Revelation 3:12)
7. To sit with Him on His throne to share His delegated authority (Revelation 3:21)

In Heaven's perfect timing, "sons of the Kingdom" will be commissioned with the mandate to bring in the most prodigious harvest of all time. Among the various harvest festivals of Israel, is the Feast of Firstfruits. The firstfruits of the harvest were collected and dedicated to the Lord as an offering to assure God's favor for the great harvest.

God commanded Israel to observe this feast to acknowledge

the fertility of the Promised Land. They were required to gather a portion of the ripe harvest and present it to the priest so he could wave the sheaf before the Lord for His acceptance and blessing.

In the same way the firstfruits offering is presented to the Lord to gain His favor for the great harvest, Jesus was the firstfruits from the dead to guarantee the great harvest or ingathering, at the end of the age.

This symbolism portrays the current season. Like the spies of Israel, pioneers and forerunners will cross over into God's promise to apprehend the reality of resurrection life and power and introduce it to the body at large. They will personally experience the reality of Hebrews 6:5 to have "...tasted the good word of God and the powers of the age to come." Their walk with the Lord and powerful ministry will usher in the latter-day anointing that will gather the greatest harvest of souls ever witnessed.

This new wave of extraordinary prophetic and power ministries will require lifestyles that facilitate favor with both God and man. There is a way to walk under God's blessings so you are producing an atmosphere attractive to people while at the same time not yielding to a "man pleasing" spirit. Paul once acknowledged that if he were still trying to please people, he would not be Christ's bondservant.

Nevertheless, spiritual anointing and favor can be apprehended and cultivated so as to leave an indelible mark on this generation. With God's favor, "sons of the Kingdom" can and should be leaders in every field. The Spirit of the Creator resides within us to awaken our senses and stimulate us beyond our natural limitations.

FAVOR WITH GOD AND MAN

There are several profoundly simple yet vitally important questions that we, and others, have been asking the Lord regarding this transition.

1. What are God's expectations of us?
2. What are our expectations for this generation?
3. What is the currency of Heaven?
4. How can we capture God's attention?

These are fair and justifiable Bible questions with anointed and strategic Bible answers.

King Solomon was the wisest, and among the most anointed leaders ever to walk the face of the earth, with the single exception of Jesus. God's Spirit outlined through him a key secret to leadership success, which is the same trait that fulfills the Lord's expectations and positions us to be used significantly by Him in His blueprint.

> Kindness and truth keep a king,
> And he hath supported by kindness his throne.
> —Proverbs 20:28, YLT

Kindness and truth are indispensable ingredients in God's formula to awaken this generation and gain divine favor. The Holy Spirit has been emphatically punctuating this reality in recent days. If we embody and convey the Lord's meekness, we will also share in His power; if we share in His obedience, we will also share in His resurrection.

THE EXAMPLE OF MOSES

As leader of Israel, Moses, described in Scripture as the meekest man in the land, stood on the brink of inheriting long-awaited promises. However, to his credit, he was not simply satisfied to experience God's promises; he also longed for His presence. His example implicates the unwise ability to walk in our prophetic promises without the Lord's presence.

Furthermore, Moses' heart was still not fully satisfied with experiencing the Lord's promise and presence; he also desired to see His glory. These should also be our expectations and longings. As the Lord passed before Moses in His goodness, He proclaimed:

> ...The Lord! the Lord! a God merciful and gracious, slow to anger, and abundant in loving-kindness and truth, keeping mercy and loving-kindness for thousands, forgiving iniquity and transgression and sin, but Who will by no means clear the guilty, visiting the iniquity of the fathers upon the children and the children's children, to the third and fourth generation.
> —Exodus 34:6–7, AMP

It is God's very nature to be filled with kindness and truth.

CAPTURING GOD'S ATTENTION

In 1995 I had an instructional dream in which I was allowed to observe one of the prominent leaders of the Latter Rain Revival. In fact, this leader was credited with launching this incredible move of God for that generation.

The Holy Spirit accomplished tremendous things through this humble man; in fact, such notable miracles occurred that a number of historians consider the demonstration of God's Spirit through him to be the greatest since the early Church. Literally millions of people were impacted with the Lord's salvation, healing, and deliverance in his ministry and others the Lord touched through him.

What about him captured the Lord's attention? What qualities did he possess that qualified him for this important assignment and provided Heaven's currency? I asked those questions prior to having the dream.

As I watched this man speaking in the dream, I noticed around his neck what looked like a leather string with a horseshoe-shaped emblem attached to it resting on his chest. Periodically, he would place the perfectly fitted figure in his mouth, as though it were a part of him, and when he did, incredible spiritual truth flowed from him. In essence, whatever this emblem represented, it allowed him to be God's mouthpiece on the earth. Many such individuals articulate God's heart for a generation. The Church is called to be Heaven's representation. We are ambassadors for Christ empowered with both anointing and authority to delegate His Kingdom. Yet certain qualities are essential to possess in order to amplify the level of empowerment we convey. I intuitively knew the item around his neck symbolized traits he possessed that provided one of the secrets to his success with God.

I was then given the following Scripture to validate the dream's spiritual application, saying:

> Do not let kindness and truth leave you;
> Bind them around your neck
> Write them on the tablet of your heart.
> So you will find favor and good repute
> In the sight of God and man.
>
> —Proverbs 3:3–4

It was evident in the dream that the marriage between kindness and truth provided a platform for God's anointing to flourish through this man. He somehow shared in the Lord's nature, which allowed him to be entrusted with tremendous spiritual power and authority. In Heaven's economy, character is the currency that will capture the Lord's attention; these attributes provide a forum for favor with both God and mankind.

KINDNESS AND TRUTH

The Spirit of Wisdom exhorts us never to forget kindness and truth. They are to be worn like a necklace and written upon the tablets of our hearts so we will walk positioned in favor before God and the people of our generation.

Many have authority with people but very little authority with God. Others have developed a vertical relationship with God but have limited avenues with people. Cultivating unfailing virtues of kindness and truth can provide both.

An adornment around the neck represents valuable insignia. We often wear jewelry and precious gems to display them as tokens of our stature. The qualities of kindness and truth are meant to be worn around our neck to reflect how dear they are to our spiritual stature.

In ancient times, people customarily wrote what was most sacred to them on pieces of parchment and wore them around their necks as a constant reminder of their personal value. In like fashion, kindness and truth are to be inscribed upon the tablets of our hearts. The human heart is a reflection of our core existence. Whatever has been written upon our heart transcribes into all we say and do.

I am not referring to mere intellectual understanding of language or mechanical repetition of words without regard to their meaning. Instead, these intrinsic qualities must influence and be absorbed into our very existence; all our words and actions then become galvanized with kindness and truth.

UNDERSTANDING KINDNESS AND TRUTH
The Hebrew word for "kindness" used in Proverbs 3:3–4, *checed*, often translated "mercy", appears 240 times in the Old Testament and is one of the most important aspects in understanding God's nature. It incorporates not only the attribute of kindness and mercy but as importantly, compassion and loyalty.

Paul discovered the secrets to access God's heart like few others in history. He advised:

So, as those who have been chosen of God, holy and
beloved, put on a heart of compassion, kindness,
humility, gentleness and patience; bearing with one
another, and forgiving each other, whoever has a
complaint against anyone; just as the Lord forgave you,
so also should you. Beyond all these things put on love,
which is the perfect bond of unity.

—Colossians 3:12–14

Someone once claimed "kindness is free." Founding father
William Penn is credited with remarking, "I expect to pass through
life but once. If, therefore, there be any kindness I can show, or
any good thing I can do, to any fellow being, let me do it now, and
not defer or neglect it, as I shall not pass this way again."

It costs us nothing to show kindness to others. It constitutes an
individual choice to pursue God's nature. Kindness is a requisite
attribute highlighted in God's Word as characteristic of His end-
time army (2 Peter 1:4).

Emeth, the Hebrew word for "truth," conveys the idea of true
testimony, while also representing the qualities of faithfulness,
reliability to one's word, and stability.

Truth is God's seal. The Spirit of Truth will guide us into all
truth and thereby eliminate all forms of deliberate falsehood
and hypocrisy.

ADORNED IN HOLY ATTIRE

Kindness and truth are essential moral qualities to gain favor
before God and humankind. They must be embraced and
cultivated in order for us to carry God's full spiritual impartation
of salvation and power. Peter identifies a heart pleasing to the
Lord when he instructed:

Do not let your adornment be merely outward—

arranging the hair, wearing gold, or putting on fine
apparel—rather let it be the hidden person of the heart,
with the incorruptible beauty of a gentle and quiet
spirit, which is very precious in the sight of God.

—1 Peter 3:3–4, NKJV

Although this passage was directed primarily to the women of
his day, it accurately conveys the principle of internal adornment
that is pleasing to God. External beauty avails little in God's eyes,
but the hidden person of the heart endowed with the imperishable
qualities of a gentle and quiet spirit are precious in His sight—they
are Heaven's currency to help us transition into the new day that
is dawning.

Church history chronicles the lives of numerous men and
women who changed their generation by applying these Kingdom
principles. All spiritual barometers indicate we are presently
positioned before a door of opportunity to facilitate tremendous
change and advancement. Now is the time to prepare our hearts
and discover God's favor to steward what is coming.

CHAPTER

5

Another Great Awakening

Early in the sixteenth century, Martin Luther nailed his
Ninety Five Theses to the church doors in Wittenberg,
Germany. This act spurred a spiritual transformation that
changed the face of Christianity, leading to the Great Awakening
of the eighteenth century. Something equally as significant is
poised to erupt today.

God's present-day dealings will ignite another "great
awakening." However, this version of Heaven's wake-up call will
quicken individuals to their personal destiny and emphasize
awareness of God's provision for the harvest of the ages. Kingdom
principles will be launched and implemented to expedite this
passage as in Jonathan Edwards Great Awakening. Edwards
recognized that human history has been a progressive journey
perpetually leading to the Person of Jesus. He also understood
that the revivals of his day were only a foretaste of something
greater to come.

His messages clearly defined God's standards which delineated
various intervals of revival and spiritual awakening producing

both times of promotion and seasons of hiding. We are now broaching an opportunity for great advancement, in which our mind-set is shifting from a defensive to an offensive posture.

In *The Works of Jonathan Edwards, Volume One, Part IV,* Edwards concluded from his analysis of Church history and God's dealings with mankind that "Time after time, when religion seemed to be almost gone, then God granted a revival, and sent some angel, or raised up some eminent person, to be an instrument of their reformation." We are overdue for a visitation such as Edwards described.

SCHOOLS OF MINISTRY

Our twenty-first century awakening will center on hidden mysteries awaiting discovery by our generation. Those who live the life of an overcomer will be allowed to eat of the hidden manna. The Spirit of Truth will quicken in this generation an allotted portion of God's Word to awaken us to divine destiny and allow us to walk in the powers of the age to come.

Truth is often hidden in plain view. Scriptural truth has many layers and at best we understand them only partially. The words are patently before us, yet their full meaning has been veiled or hidden. For centuries archaeologists meticulously scrutinized the ancient writings and hieroglyphics encrypted on Egyptian artifacts. Only with the discovery of the Rosetta Stone was a glossary of ancient language furnished to interpret the mysteries.

For hundreds of years Jewish followers contemplated the prophetic Scriptures pointing to their Messiah and the restoration of Israel, yet none understood their application. The Lord's crucifixion, burial, and resurrection exemplifies a mystery hidden in plain view. Scripture recorded the message, but only in its fulfillment did absolute understanding develop.

Now some end-time mysteries foreseen by Daniel and John

(Daniel 12; Revelation10) are being disclosed and imparted as a righteous generation anointed with revelatory insight probes deep into God's heart where they are hidden. Schools of ministry to prepare and equip the Body of Christ for this notable destiny are emerging with an amplified sense of responsibility.

UNLOCKING MYSTERIES

In 1799, outside the seaside town of Rosetta, Egypt, leaders of Napoleon's army uncovered a granite stone. The relic, known as the Rosetta Stone, dates to 196 B.C. On the stone a message is inscribed in three discernible scripts–hieroglyphics, demotic, and Greek. Archaeologists surmise this was done so priests, government officials, and rulers in Egypt could all understand it.

During that era, religious documentation was preserved with hieroglyphics, the common script of the Egyptian populace was demotic, and Greek was the language used by Egyptian rulers. The Greek translation supplied a tool for archaeologists to decode the other two communications.

The key to crack the code was discovered, providing a language glossary to help translate many other ancient Egyptian writings. Centuries passed with the message remaining undecipherable until acquisition of the Rosetta Stone provided the key to decipher the messages. The documentation had always been plainly visible, but their comprehension had been locked behind an unknown door.

Today, the Spirit of Revelation is imparting keys of interpretation and supernatural insight. Biblical passages have been before us all along, but our spiritual comprehension has been painfully limited. Thankfully, the Holy Spirit's release of insight with understanding will assist in this prophetic journey. The finest wine has been reserved for the latter days.

GOD'S LIGHTHOUSES

Many are being trained to experience releases of spiritual light on a level unseen since the first century apostles, while numerous individuals and ministries are being positioned to offer revelatory insight that will effectively direct our spiritual paths and sanctify our souls. In Psalm 24, David asks, "Who may ascend into the hill of the Lord? Or who may stand in His holy place?"

The answer is clear cut! Those with clean hands, a pure heart, and who have not lifted up their souls to falsehood nor sworn deceitfully! This denotes those who have not embraced a lie for the truth and pledged allegiance to what is false. The Spirit of Truth is manifesting in our generation to alleviate this divisive predicament, which will be a primary function of the storehouses operating as ministry schools to mentor future leaders for this cause. Our job is to call upon Him, and He promises to answer and show us wonderful things of His Kingdom.

> Call to Me and I will answer you and show you great and mighty things, fenced in and hidden, which you do not know (do not distinguish and recognize, have knowledge of and understand).
> —Jeremiah 33:3, AMP

Jesus prayed to His Father, "Sanctify them in the truth; Your word is truth. As You sent Me into the world, I also have sent them into the world" (John 17:17–18). Truth that has not yet been fully understood or distinguishable will be uncovered and apprehended in this day. The Lord is approaching us with an open book in His hand beckoning us to consume it. When we eat His Book of Truth, its contents meld with our spiritual composition, weaving end-time truth into our spiritual DNA (Revelation10:8). It is the book of redemption and the revelation of Jesus Christ.

A VOICE FROM THE PAST

Maria Woodworth-Etter was one of the most well-known and highly regarded evangelists at the turn of the twentieth century. For four decades, with great integrity and faithful stewardship, she successfully presented the gospel of salvation through demonstrations of the Spirit and His power.

Shortly thereafter, Woodworth-Etter preached a message on restored truth in the end-time, built around several visions and revelations she had received from the Lord. In her experiences she was shown how masses of religious leaders and teachers would display a form of godliness, but ultimately deny God's power and revelatory mantles.

The Lord conveyed to her that many false teachers would emerge in the last days in far worse condition than the first century Scribes and Pharisees. The Lord also showed her that sin and unbelief in our day would exceed the first century rejection of truth, because we are living at a time of more light. She also prophesied that people would willingly embrace blindness and follow teachers who hide behind a refuge of lies, false doctrines, and human traditions.

On March 24, 1904, Woodworth-Etter was taken in a vision to see God's heart for the last day outpouring. She witnessed a hand descending from Heaven symbolic of God's manifest power exhibited in the last-day generation to a body of people prepared for it. She was informed of an approaching season when judgment would begin in the household of faith to separate the wheat from the tares. Then, the Lord said to her, He would send meat in due season to the hungry and thirsty.

She was allowed to witness how God's hand would move vigorously in the end-of-the-ages saints, sealing a company of people with His power, glory, and revelatory truth. The final outcome would be the unveiling of the Father's lavish love and an impartation of divine wisdom and supernatural knowledge regarding His ultimate plan for the ages. She was told it would mark the winding up of the harvest of the ages, the preparation of a bridal company, and the closing of the Gentile door. Although she felt a portion of this vision applied to her generation, the fullness will be achieved in our day.

PRAYER MOUNTAIN

For more than a decade, the Lord has been speaking prophetically that He intends to escalate the West's intercessory prayer emphasis. The Holy Spirit expressly promised that an impartation of grace for intercession would be transferred from the South Korean Prayer Mountain. As a result, numerous "houses of prayer" and "harp and bowl" type ministries have emerged in response to this prophetic call, with the result that twenty-four hour-a-day prayer is now a reality in our nation.

With our ministry, the Lord symbolically portrayed shipping navigation to communicate portions of His strategy in this area. He is presently training lighthouses to furnish abundant light to leader-ships to direct navigation through these perilous times. They will be lighthouses of prayer and revelatory insight serving to uncover submerged obstructions and prevent shipwreck.

A lighthouse is defined as a structure along coastal waters to guide ships by day as a land marker and to project light during darkness. Lighthouses are primarily constructed at strategic points to mark harbor entrances. They help ascertain a ship's location and warn of potential hazards. Each of these functions has a spiritual counterpart.

Substantial spiritual Light is about to be released in God's house. This inspired revelatory truth will highlight God's promises for this generation and direct us to havens of rest. His Light dispels darkness and exposes the adversary's schemes to promote shipwreck. The spiritual lighthouses will impart great understanding and wisdom crucial in accomplishing our prophetic mandates.

IGNITING PASSION

The ministry schools assigned to this task will be commissioned to ignite passion in the believer's hearts and to train them as spiritual warriors. The last century birthed three significant expressions of revival according to this model.

During the spring of 1900, the weight of God began to burden Charles Parham. He discerned something spiritually fresh on the horizon which inspired a yeaning in him for greater personal manifestations of God's power. Consequently, he withdrew from the evangelistic field, gathered a small company of consecrated students from his Topeka, Kansas, ministry school, and for the remainder of the year they devoted themselves to prayer and prophetic proclamation of God's promises in His Word.

Then on December 31, 1900, while the group was fervently praying together, one student encountered God as the 120 had on the Day of Pentecost. This reintroduction to the Spirit's infilling spurred the Pentecostal Age, which has now swept the nations of the earth.

In like fashion, Evan Roberts overcame personal hardship in his passion to become a preacher. Despite his lack of education, Roberts entered the Newcastle Emlyn ministry school. A bright flame burned in his heart for intimate relationship with the Lord and his desperation found expression through extended seasons of prayer. By the spring of 1904, Roberts experienced breakthrough and encountered the Lord in an experiential way. Recounting the experience to his friend Sydney Evans, he shared how he had seen the entire nation of Wales lifted to Heaven, and God promised him a hundred thousand Welsh souls. Thus a revival was born.

Nearly a half century later, on February 12, 1948, at the North Battleford, Saskatchewan, Sharon School of Ministry, the Canadian Latter Rain Revival was birthed. After attending a 1947 William

Branham healing meeting in Vancouver, British Columbia, they returned with a passion for revival in their own region. Leaders at the school had spent the previous year in a season of consecration, fasting, and prayer and the Holy Spirit answered with a mighty outpouring. According to leader Ern Hawtin:

> "God moved in the students midst in a strange new manner. Some students were under the power of God on the floor, others were kneeling in adoration and worship before the Lord. The anointing deepened until the awe of God was upon everyone. The Lord spoke to one of the brethren saying, "Go and lay hands upon a certain student and pray for him." While he was in doubt and contemplation, one of the sisters who had been under the power of God went to the brother saying the same words, and naming the identical student he was to pray for. He went in obedience and a revelation was given concerning the student's life and future ministry. After this a long prophecy was given with minute details concerning the great thing God was about to do. The pattern for the revival and many details concerning it were given."

Following these early events, people began to flock to North Battleford from all over North America and the world. Revival passion had been ignited and spread rapidly throughout the nations with a healing, deliverance, and Holy Spirit baptism message that paved the way for the Charismatic Renewal.

MINISTRY OF RECOVERY

The considerable insights delegated to the Church over the past decades have numerous present-day applications. These corresponding plans and strategies involve multiple spiritual deposits with fruitful Kingdom focus. Establishing ministry schools is high among the Lord's priorities, since equipping warriors for the upcoming battle will be the primary mandate. Providing thorough understanding of our spiritual heritage and victorious future will be foremost among curricula agendas, for which a divine blueprint has been progressively unfolding in recent years.

Our nation experienced tremendous expressions of spiritual visitation during the last century. In the late nineteenth century, Alexander Dowie and other prominent leaders facilitated a corporate restoration of healing ministry, while throughout the early twentieth century the Baptism in the Holy Spirit experience seized and swiftly disseminated around the nation. Throughout the early twentieth century, forerunners and pioneers blazed a global trail demonstrating the Pentecostal message, which continues to this day.

The healing revival birthed in 1946 provided one of the most incredible manifestations of God's grace ever witnessed. Theologians and Church historians verified that the intensity of God's revelation and power during those years was unequaled in modern history. I will discuss this revival much more thoroughly in the next chapter.

RELEASING BIRTHRIGHT

Each visitation illuminates spiritual birthrights in the Bible, despite which they were neither fully construed nor universally appropriated. Historically, the Lord has always had a remnant of people on the earth walking intimately with Him in Pentecostal power. Very often, that number diminished significantly in proportion to the corporate body of believers confessing faith in Christ.

For example, for hundreds of years the corporate Church did not fully enjoy the divine benefits promised in Acts 2. The infilling of the Spirit, and all its wonderful bestowals of power, have been covenant blessings since the Day of Pentecost. However, during the Dark Ages very few people experientially apprehended this reality, for though the truth was always present, their eyes were somehow veiled.

Through Charles Parham and William J. Seymour, the Lord reintroduced Holy Spirit Baptism to the corporate Church, which following the twentieth-century restoration, became recognized as fundamental to our Christian journey. Nonetheless, each revival seemed to end in shipwreck, for spiritual Light restored to the Church in each outpouring was often distorted or taken beyond biblical boundaries.

We are presently in a season of recovery! God's Light is being restored through leaders groomed and refined for this duty. Additionally, the Spirit of Revelation will introduce our eyes to what they have not yet seen and our ears to what they have not heard. Jesus taught that:

> ...every teacher and interpreter of the Sacred Writings
> who has been instructed about and trained for the
> kingdom of heaven and has become a disciple is like
> a householder who brings forth out of his storehouse
> treasure that is new and [treasure that is] old [the fresh
> as well as the familiar].
> —Matthew 13:52, AMP

These havens of restoration and release will be schools of the Spirit and lighthouses of God!

GUARDIANS AND TUTORS

"I will give lighthouses to any sincere person willing to clean them up and put light in them again," the Lord told us through prophetic utterances. "I will make them Guardians of the Truth,'" the Spirit added.

Guardians are those responsible for guarding and preserving welfare or property committed into their hands by another for protection and oversight. This is also a primary component of storehouses. We are being granted supernatural help to collect a harvest through overseers bearing spiritual authority authorized for this purpose and then to guard that harvest, assisted by angels dispatched to work alongside this company.

In spiritual terms, a guardian's duty is the stewardship and custodial care of divine impartations. Caretakers of spiritual graces become watchers and champions of the causes committed to their care.

Light is produced by merging the Word and Spirit. The letter of the law alone yields death, but mingled with the Spirit it elicits life and light. This blend generates light for the lighthouses which will be the "Guardians of the Truth!" And they must uphold a lofty standard of purity and excellence.

Through them, people who dwell in a shroud of darkness will see a great Light. Guardians of this grace will oversee the lighthouses and tutor this generation as champions and overcomers (Matthew 4:15–16).

> Then Jesus again spoke to them, saying, "I am the Light
> of the world; he who follows Me will not walk in the
> darkness, but will have the Light of life."
> —John 8:12

We are desperate for the brightness of God's Light in our spiritual houses. The illumination of God's glory will always highlight the straight and narrow path leading to His Kingdom. When our lighthouses transmit the inspired Word of the Living God—Word and Spirit integrated as one; they will then reflect His glory and our schools of the Spirit will teach God's thoughts and ways.

DIVINE REVELATION

An allegorical vision given to us in 1994 portrayed an old neglected temple awaiting refurbishment. The temple interior had been vandalized, and the roof's poor condition provided inadequate covering.

The temple is a prophetic analogy of prior revivals and spiritual outpouring that functioned fruitfully once for a season but was lost. The work of vandals represented evil spirits causing disruption and mayhem. Unfortunately, they found access into the purposes. The inadequate roof represented a lack of prayer covering. Isaiah fortold:

> "In a favorable time I have answered you, and in a day
> of salvation I have helped you; and I will keep you and
> give you for a covenant of the people, to restore the
> land, to make them inherit the desolate heritages…"
> —Isaiah 49:8

The Spirit is presently breathing on lost heritage. Unfulfilled commissions and mantles of revelation and power are available to be apprehended. Heavenly directives are being re-commissioned with fresh purpose and stewardship. Temple restoration is the primary objective of the new occupancy and the roof's renovation with adequate prayer covering is essential. God's temples are to become houses of prayer.

THINGS BOTH OLD AND NEW

The treasures delegated from spiritual storehouses will be revelatory truths, both new and old. We will bring forward the delegation of truth imparted to prior generations as well as release Kingdom mysteries and secrets set apart for this age. It will be a consolidation of the fresh mingled with the familiar.

The important aspect of these revelations is their application to our current place in Church history. Jesus assured that a generation would perform the "greater works" (John 14:12). These will be the "sons of the Kingdom" who carry the Sevenfold Spirit of God that rested upon Jesus in His perfect example of a Son of the Kingdom.

The Lord once told Nathanael that he would witness great demonstrations of His power and authority, which was fulfilled when the heavens opened for him to observe angels ascending and descending upon the Son of Man (John 1:50–51). We should be so familiar with the spiritual arena that we perceive the angelic host ascending and descending upon the "sons of the Kingdom" in fulfillment of God's redemptive plan.

QUALIFICATION FOR DUTY

The apostle Paul identified a qualification needed to equip us with power to perform heavenly duties when he prayed:

> ...Giving thanks to the Father, who has qualified us to share in the inheritance of the saints in Light.
> —Colossians 1:12

How do we know if we are called or qualified for this mandate? The Bible assures us that just as the Spirit has instructed us, so shall we abide in Him (1 John 2:27).

1. What has been the Holy Spirit's instruction in your life?
2. Does your heart burn desperately for God?
3. Has He for many years released understanding and training to you concerning the walk of intimacy and the ministry of revival and power?
4. Has He been putting His finger on issues of your soul that

are potential snares of the adversary?
5. Has grace been released to extract those strongholds?

Clearly, we are neither adequate nor qualified in ourselves. Our adequacy comes from God, who has qualified us as servants of His new covenant (2 Corinthians 3:5–6). A decree from God's heart is seeking to enlist an army for Kingdom purpose and to establish His governmental design. Apostles, prophets, evangelists, pastors, and teachers are being summoned to their posts of duty.

Ministry schools are being charged with heavenly authority to equip leaders, who, once in place and functioning in proper biblical order, will enable God's glory to descend upon the temple as in Solomon's day. Then hidden secrets and Kingdom mysteries will become a living reality.

God's Word will be the cornerstone of our revelations, as well as the validation of all our end-time promises, and we will understand it more thoroughly in this hour than any prior generation, for this is the age of the fulfillment of all revelations. This will be the feast of the open book.

CHAPTER

6

As I was with Moses

I t has been said, "We live in the present, we dream of the future, and we learn eternal truths from the past." Major intersections throughout the centuries have transformed an entire generation and changed the course of human history. We are at the precipice of perhaps one of the greatest transformations since the days of the early Church.

To satisfactorily grasp a shift of this nature requires measurable understanding of our heritage, particularly in regard to modern Pentecostalism. God does nothing without a cause. He has very deliberately been orchestrating spiritual outpourings over the last one hundred years, as well as incredible supernatural expressions globally of biblical proportions, much of which the modern Church has unfortunately overlooked. The Welsh Revival, Azusa Street, and contemporary apostolic restoration revivals provide wonderful lessons to help prepare us to move forward into the next installment.

Nevertheless, another great awakening is on the horizon to bring an army out of the wilderness. Soldiers in this army will have eyes illumined and hearts enlightened to comprehend God's strategy and apprehend Heaven's design for the latter days.

MODERN PENTECOST

The Welsh Revival was a profound spiritual awakening. From late 1904 until early 1905, the Holy Spirit's outpouring in Wales directly impacted one hundred thousand souls for the Kingdom of Heaven and inspired countless millions.

Few revivals have been so well documented and thoroughly considered as the Welsh Revival. One young ministry student, Evan Roberts, is principally credited with launching this wonderful expression of God's heart. God's Spirit strongly influenced an entire region, transforming it virtually overnight through this young man's desperation for God.

Roberts was in the Newcastle Emlyn ministry school when the Holy Spirit fell upon him, igniting the 1904 outpouring. He had been discovering God in significant ways in the months preceding his entrance to the school. However, two weeks after arriving at the school He had a God encounter. The resulting empowering of the Spirit transformed Roberts into a revivalist who altered the spiritual atmosphere of Wales.

The Welsh Revival generated wonderful fruit, but that fruit is merely a token of the significant demonstration of God's Spirit imminently poised to be released in the earth. Nevertheless, stewards of this move of God must undergo considerable preparation to favorably usher in the coming grace for revelation and power.

Frank Bartleman was also one of the earliest influences in the twentieth century Pentecostal outpouring. He knew about discerning times and seasons and spiritual transition, which he wrote of in *Azusa Street: The Roots of Modern-day Pentecostalism*. He said, "The present Pentecostal manifestation did not break out in a moment, like a huge prairie fire, and set the world on fire. In fact no work of God ever appears that way. There is a necessary time for preparation...men may wonder where it came from, not being conscious of the preparation, but there is always such."

Many believers have devoted themselves to the lessons learned from the Welsh Revival and others like it, and incredible preparatory advances have been made in recent years.

For those positioned to apprehend it, a heavenly door is about to be opened wide in these transitional days.

VISITING WALES

In August 2005, Wanda and I were conducting a conference in Bridgend, Wales, a region we found genuinely invigorating to hold meetings at because of its historical importance, especially since a substantial portion of our ministry has been devoted to understanding prior expressions of spiritual outpouring and their contemporary relevance. I had already shared in the meetings our message on modern Church history and the seeds of revival sown for the present Pentecostal movement.

Part of the time line I shared there is as follows:

1885

Bethshan Conference on Holiness and Healing, London, England; Led by William Boardman and A. B. Simpson.

Many historians acknowledge that the present Pentecostal movement was first initiated in this June 1885 meeting. Alexander Dowie and others pointed to the London conference as the seedbed for the healing movement they enjoyed. This conference laid the foundation for the corporate restoration of the Spirit's infilling and the activation of spiritual gifts.

Some reports acknowledge that as many as two thousand leaders converged in London to discover that divine healing is the "children's bread." A. B. Simpson first visited William Boardman's healing houses in London and brought the concept back to the United States, which was popularized by Alexander Dowie in Zion, Illinois.

1896

Alexander Dowie commissioned his Apostolic Church and founded the city of Zion, Illinois, a few years later. His entire ministry was built upon great demonstrations of healing and deliverance. He was a prolific author and a steward of spiritual truth which he circulated internationally through his publication *Leaves of Healing*. Unfortunately, his later years were obscured by controversy and deception when he made the well documented "Elijah proclamation," in which he claimed to be Elijah the Restorer. Even so, he was a great pioneer of the faith to whom we owe a huge debt of gratitude.

Gordon Lindsay, in his periodical, *Voice of Healing*, honored Dowie and acknowledged him as a "stalwart preacher who proclaimed Jesus Christ both Savior and Healer." Lindsay states that, "In a single-handed crusade in Chicago, and against great odds, Dr. Dowie established the right to pray for the sick without interference from civil authorities. Tens of thousands testified of healing under this man's ministry and his work was without a parallel in his day."

No other ministry at that time did more to facilitate the healing movement to so many people worldwide than Alexander Dowie. At the turn of the twentieth century he even prophesied the future role radio and television would have as vehicles for spreading the message of God's Kingdom.

1900

Initially a revivalist with a very successful soul-winning work, Charles Parham was used mightily to help launch the twentieth century Church into her destiny. His ministry became spiritually pregnant with something he could not fully articulate; therefore, he withdrew from the evangelistic field to a house of prayer in Topeka, Kansas, to discover what this beckoning of God's Spirit was.

Many of his contemporaries criticized this decision, implying he had lost his burden for souls, but it was actually his spiritual hunger that drove him to the house of prayer. Oftentimes, divine destiny is conceived amid misunderstanding and opposition.

He and a small group of mature leaders started the Bethel School of Ministry. Meanwhile, from the spring of 1900 until December 31, 1900, they contended for the birthing of this new thing he sought. Then, on New Year's Eve 1901 it happened: The Holy Spirit descended in this prayer meeting on Mrs. Agnes Ozman and expressed Himself as He had on the 120 on the Day of Pentecost two thousand years ago.

Charles Parham had already been impacting a sizable number of people regionally as a revivalist, but when he birthed this fresh expression of God's Kingdom, the release touched the nations. This principle clearly distinguishes between a "Church" perspective and the Kingdom vision.

1904–1905

Evan Roberts launched the Welsh Revival, setting the stage for the Azusa Street Revival, under the leadership of William J. Seymour. Roberts was born in 1878 and lived his early days as a miner and blacksmith. A passionate fire burned in his soul for the Lord until it found expression in the revival. He is credited with changing much in the traditions of the day with extended times of praise and worship and a de-emphasis on preaching. He would often abandon sermons with interruptions of worship and intercession. He stressed the importance of God's Spirit and spontaneity in responding to His leadership.

Although the Welsh outpouring most likely did not accomplish the fullness of its mandate, it left an indelible mark on this generation's perception of community transformation.

1906
Frank Bartleman was a man who carried a spiritual burden for Los Angeles, and, having heard about Charles Parham's ministry and also the Welsh Revival, along with others desired the same and began to contend for the destiny of their city.

While Bartleman was praying in Los Angeles, the Lord was preparing the answer to his prayer in Houston, Texas, through a most unusual man: William J. Seymour, an African American Nazarene pastor, who was attending Charles Parham's Bible Training School and was captured by God's Spirit despite having to battle the evils of racism. Seymour accepted the invitation to go to Los Angeles to pastor a small church. As he began teaching from Acts 2, many individuals received the Holy Spirit's infilling.

By mid-1906 it became necessary to move into a larger facility at 312 Azusa Street, where the Holy Spirit continued His work and attracted people from around the world. Men and women from all races, walks of life, and socioeconomic positions flooded the little mission.

What transpired in this little run-down mission on Azusa Street in Los Angeles, California, though termed a revival, in reality was much more! It was another unfolding of God's redemptive plan and a revolution from the current Church paradigms.

1910
John G. Lake returned to Spokane, Washington, after spending five years in Africa as a missionary and apostolic leader. While in South Africa, he birthed numerous churches, and tremendous displays of the miraculous took place. In Spokane, Lake opened "houses of healing," where one hundred thousand supernatural healings within five years were recorded.

Great hunger permeated the hearts of the people during this incredible spiritual awakening. In articulating his observations, however, Lake reiterated that people appeared more captured by the phenomena of God rather than the Person.

1933

In a June baptismal service on the Ohio River, an amazing and thoroughly documented phenomenon occurred. While baptizing the seventeenth person, before a crowd in excess of four thousand, a whirling blaze of fire descended above William Branham. Witnesses reported the sound of rushing wind as all experienced the incredible event. Many of the witnesses ran in fear; others knelt in prayer and worship. A voice spoke from the fire saying, "As John the Baptist was the forerunner of the first coming of Christ, so you will bring a message that is the forerunner of the second coming of Christ."

Numerous news organizations picked up the story and circulated it around the U.S. and Canada. One headline read, "Mysterious Light Appears over Baptist Minister While Baptizing in the Ohio River." *The Jeffersonville Evening News* reported the incident with the subheading, "Mysterious Star Appears over Minister While Baptizing." Though many may debate the full meaning of the event, its authenticity is not disputed.

1946–1956

Following the deaths of several of the previous generation's spiritual giants, such as Smith Wigglesworth, Charles Price, and Aimee Semple McPherson, William Branham received an angelic visitation that thrust him into the forefront as a pioneer of the Latter Rain Revival. Many of the revival's eventual leaders were inspired by and commissioned in Branham meetings. By 1948 the entire world seemed to be experiencing some measure of the healing revival.

1956

America turns down her opportunity. For ten years the Holy Spirit demonstrated Heaven's supernatural virtue with tremendous miracles, signs, and wonders, yet no corporate repentance or turning to God resulted. Many came out to embrace God's blessings, but not the Person. John G. Lake's 1925 assessment that, "The people embraced the phenomena of God but not the Person" had repeated itself.

1962–63

In December 1962, William Branham publicly shared his visionary experience in which he found himself standing in a desert area. He then heard a loud blast and watched as seven angels descended from Heaven with great power and authority. This message was taped and on record before the events that transpired early 1963.

While hunting javelina in Sunset Mountain Arizona, in the spring of 1963, William Branham was visited by seven angels who descended with such force that it literally created the sound of a sonic boom and dislodged rocks and boulders in the Mountain region. Many witnesses heard the resulting sound. The seven angels commissioned William Branham to preach understanding from the Book of Revelation. The visitation fulfilled the vision shared in 1962. It was further documented as an authentic spiritual encounter when the seven angels left the region leaving a mysterious ring in the Arizona sky.

Numerous secular scientific and news periodicals carried photos and articles of the strange cloud including *Life* magazine, *Science* magazine, *The Arizona Republic*, The University of Arizona, *Weatherwise Magazine*, and many others. The headline in the May 1963 issue of *Life* magazine read, "What Is This Mysterious Ring?" To this day no natural explanation can be given for the mysterious ring that resulted in the Arizona sky and remained illuminated thirty minutes past sunset.

Something transpired at Sunset Mountain. Could it be that God did just what Brother Branham said, and sent seven angels to that generation, and if so, what are the implications for us?

1977

On January 21, Roland Buck, an Assembly of God pastor in Boise, Idaho, had a supernatural encounter with God that transformed the remainder of his life and inaugurated a series of messages direct from God's heart. This encounter fulfilled a 1933 prophetic prediction indicating 1977 would be a pivotal transition year.

Following this experience, the angel Gabriel appeared to Pastor Buck twenty seven times over the following two and one-half years. This point in time marked a significant shift in the Spirit realm from a "church age" mentality into a more pronounced Kingdom revelation as demonstrated by the Lord Jesus and the early apostles.

VISITING MORIAH CHAPEL

Naturally, while in Wales, Wanda and I looked forward to visiting Moriah Chapel and the site of the Welsh Revival. We arranged for a tour with the local custodian, since that evening's service was to be our last due to an early return before Hurricane Katrina made landfall. The visit was inspiring. The elderly gentleman who served as our guide lived his entire life directly across the street from Moriah Chapel and warmly and enthusiastically shared incredible testimonies and firsthand knowledge of friends and families influenced by this revival. He recalled taverns and pubs shut down because no more customers spent their hard-earned money on alcohol and promiscuity. He recounted how jails were no longer filled with criminals but transformed into community centers serving the revival. The entire region was transfigured under the spirit of conviction. Even now, many local families continue to follow God as second and third-generation legacies of this revival.

I stood behind the pulpit for an extended period of time imagining how it might have looked in 1904 as the building filled with the cloud of God's presence and the altar flooded with tears of repentance. My only thought was, Lord, do it again, and more! Afterward we returned to Bridgend for our last service.

MOSES MY SERVANT IS DEAD

That evening during worship, I was contemplating what I was going to share as the culminating message of the conference. I wanted to leave the people with a spiritual deposit of hope and restoration regarding their heritage. As my mind focused on this objective, I heard the Lord's voice telling me, "Moses my servant is dead." That statement immediately quickened in my mind the passage in His Word saying:

> And he [Moses] said to them, "I am a hundred and
> twenty years old today; I am no longer able to come and
> go, and the LORD has said to me, 'You shall not cross
> this Jordan.' It is the LORD your God who will cross
> ahead of you; He will destroy these nations before you,
> and you shall dispossess them. Joshua is the one who
> will cross ahead of you, just as the LORD has spoken."
> —Deuteronomy 31:2–3

With that realization I then heard the Lord ask, "How long has it been since the seeds for the modern Pentecostal movement were sown?" As often as I had preached the historical account of the last century's spiritual heritage, I had never actually done the math. I calculated in my mind that since this was the year 2005 and the beginning was 1885, it had been a hundred and twenty years. I realized then that the Moses Era was over. We had been called out but had not yet crossed over.

The Lord is speaking to this generation that:

"Moses My servant is dead. Now therefore, arise, go
over this Jordan, you and all this people, to the land
which I am giving to them—the children of Israel.
Every place that the sole of your foot will tread upon
I have given you, as I said to Moses...No man shall be
able to stand before you all the days of your life; as I
was with Moses, so I will be with you. I will not leave
you nor forsake you."
                                        —Joshua 1:2–3, 5, NKJV

The season of transition is upon us, and a new commissioning
is about to be announced in the order of Joshua.

THE MOSES GENERATION

The one hundred twenty years of spiritual activity between 1885
and 2005 have functioned in the order of Moses. Undoubtedly,
Moses was one of God's greatest men in history. His intimate
friendship with the Lord set a standard we aspire to today. Even
so, the totality of his original mandate was not fully achieved in
his lifetime.

Moses brought the people out of Egypt under God's mighty
hand of power through miracles, signs, and wonders; but that
generation did not cross over into their destiny.

According to Deuteronomy 29:4, they did not possess the
revelatory anointing essential to cooperate with God. Their eyes
and ears were not opened and their hearts were not devoted to the
revelation of Heaven's plan. As a result, they were disqualified,
and a season of discipline ensued.

Nevertheless, the next generation followed with spiritual
hunger and desperation that captured Heaven's attention and
positioned them for their inheritance. That is the same model

we have witnessed over the last century. Naturally, that is not to point a condemning finger at the saints of the prior generation. Clearly, there were many very godly people who openly embraced the fullness of God's desire. Even so, prudent historical analysis reveals that the corporate Church did not embrace the open door opportunities set before them to cross spiritual Jordan.

John G. Lake's estimation in 1925 of the mistake made in being more enthralled by God's acts than by Who He is was again repeated in the fifties. Thus, for the twenty-first century generation to cross over into a Joshua anointing will require God's abundant grace for walking intimately with Him, as well as a thorough understanding of the lessons learned from past achievements and failures. The writer of Hebrews admonishes us to:

> Remember those who led you, who spoke the word of
> God to you; and considering the result of their conduct,
> imitate their faith. Jesus Christ is the same yesterday
> and today and forever.
>
> —Hebrews 13:7–8

This Scripture admonishes us to remember and be constantly mindful of those who have gone before us. Furthermore, we are to consider well and observe accurately the end of their lives. This examination positions us to imitate their faith. In so doing, the Lord will do through us what he did through them by mighty expressions of His power and authority—because He is the same yesterday, today, and forever.

The Lord promised Joshua that He would walk with him as He had with Moses. Our assurance is the same. As the Lord accompanied the mighty champions of the last century, so also will He be with us. Even so, what we do may appear totally different. Joshua's accomplishments were distinctly different from those of Moses.

IN THE ORDER OF MOSES

Following the Holy Spirit's outpouring at Azusa Street, our nation witnessed one of the greatest spiritual awakenings since the Day of Pentecost. The 1946–56 Latter Rain Revival was unprecedented on multiple levels. We have written on this subject in various articles and will not take the space here to enumerate the many wonderful things God did. The important aspect for this text is the original commissioning credited with launching this revival. All historians agree that William Branham was the predominant figure responsible for initiating this national and international healing revival.

On May 7, 1946, after a night of agonizing prayer and travail, William Branham received a visitation from an angel who delivered a divine commissioning directly from God's throne. This account has been well documented, and the revival's fruit itself testifies of its validity.

Gordon Lindsay, founder of Christ for the Nations, wrote of this spiritual experience: "The results of the angelic visitation to William Branham have been a steadily rising tide of revival that has sounded out throughout the world, and the end is not yet."

The Book of Acts plainly substantiates that angels labored closely with the early saints. God's ways have not changed. The angel said to Branham, "Fear not. I am sent from the Presence of Almighty God to tell you that your peculiar life and your misunderstood ways have been to indicate that God has sent you to take a gift of divine healing to the peoples of the world. If you will be sincere and get the people to believe you, nothing shall stand before your prayer...not even cancer!"

The angel went on to tell William Branham that he would take the ministry of healing around the world and eventually pray for kings, princes, and monarchs. Brother Branham replied, "How can this be since I am a poor man and I live among poor people and I have no education?" The angel responded, "As the prophet Moses was given two signs to prove that he was sent from God, so will you be given two signs."

For approximately thirty minutes the angel stood before Brother Branham explaining the commission and the way the ministry would operate in the supernatural arena. The important point of this teaching is that Branham's role as the principal figure launching the Latter Rain Revival was a commission in the order of Moses.

His commission and healing ministry began in 1946, and by 1948 the world was aflame with revival fire. Millions of people were saved, healed, and delivered of severe oppression by God's sovereign touch in the years following the visitation.

This exceptional demonstration of God's power was launched in the order of Moses. This past generation has been a Moses generation. We have now arrived at the end of this phase of God's plan and are about to shift into the Joshua commissioning.

THE ROLE OF THE VOICE OF HEALING

Shreveport, Louisiana, was a pivotal city in 1947, when Gordon Lindsay made the transition from Ashland, Oregon, to there. He and a businessman named Jack Moore together founded The *Voice of Healing* magazine as a tool to facilitate the revival's new outpouring of God's Spirit. Initially the primary purpose of this ministry was to organize William Branham's meetings and publicize the tremendous things God was doing in the revival. This organization's activities served as a forerunner model for much of what we will see utilized in today's ministries.

Many healing evangelists came under the The *Voice of Healing* umbrella because Gordon Lindsay's leadership provided a safety net for these individuals who were functioning in powerful demonstrations of God's healing virtue. Lindsay demanded integrity, biblical soundness, and unity of those obtaining his endorsement and oversight.

The *Voice of Healing's* mode of operation offers an embryonic pattern of many ministries that will be established as apostolic networks and God's storehouses. Relationally based alliances of this nature will help perpetuate the Holy Spirit's outpouring and provide biblical parameters for God's leadership.

The 1946–56 revival was short-lived in large part because this mechanism could not remain intact. By 1956 several ministries had received prophetic insight that the revival was over. America had turned down her opportunity! Like Israel, a season of discipline would ensue before another opportunity could be re-offered and apprehended. Like Israel, America was enamored with God's hand more than His face; both missed the day of their visitation. We cannot afford to make that tragic mistake again today!

The Lord informed one ministry leader that he "was in a rat race and even if he won the race, he was still a rat." This was a symbolic analogy of what ministry had become. For many leaders, ministry had disintegrated into a competitive exhibition to determine which evangelist had the largest tent, the most numerous crowds, or most profound miracles.

Our purpose in stating this is not to point accusatory fingers at the prior generation, but rather, to learn from their mistakes so we do not replicate them. Honestly, if these pitfalls befell those notably used righteous saints, how much more are we subject to these traps? We must therefore persist in contending for a great impartation of God's grace to alleviate these snares so we may rise above worldly spiritual influences. "Angels that gather" are being dispatched to help free us from spirits of carnality commissioned by our adversary to cause personal failure and collapse of the perpetual outpouring we are anticipating.

ALLEVIATING PAST FAILURES

For many years I aggressively studied past revivals to understand what was done properly and erroneously. I genuinely desired to comprehend how a revival as powerful as the Latter Rain healing movement could end with such despair and failure. I had studied many of the individuals used in this outpouring and discerned their initial sincerity. How could such wonderful ministries witness such incredible outpourings of God's power and yet end with discouragement and disappointment?

The Lord led me to an interesting passage in the Book of Numbers outlining, at least in part, basic understanding of this dilemma. Israel had been granted the incredible opportunity of following God's leadership and entering their land of promise. Unfortunately, ten individuals who had surveyed the land returned with evil reports. Their unbelief swayed the entire nation to reject God's destiny for them and offend His Spirit.

It was not God's goal simply to display tremendous miracles, signs, and wonders, but to utilize His power as a means of achieving His covenant promise to Abraham. The ultimate purpose was to set apart a body of people with whom He would fellowship and fulfill His mandate. That is ours as well! Like the Israelites, the prior generation embraced God's healing power and relished the signs and wonders, yet missed the purpose for which they were delegated. As a result, the Lord instructed Moses to announce His discipline and their lost opportunity. He said:

> "Surely you shall not come into the land in which I swore
> to settle you, except Caleb the son of Jephunneh and
> Joshua the son of Nun. Your children, however, whom
> you said would become a prey—I will bring them in, and
> they will know the land which you have rejected. But as
> for you, your corpses will fall in this wilderness."
> —Numbers 14:30–32

However, the next morning the people decided they would pursue the Promised Land after all. Moses warned that he as the prophetic voice would not go with them nor would the Ark of the Covenant. They had neither the revelatory insight nor God's manifest presence essential to apprehend the promise. Consequently, the Amalakites rose against God's people and thoroughly defeated them.

The prior generation experienced much of the same pattern. A pronouncement was proclaimed that America had turned down her opportunity; however, a group continued to perpetuate the revival without clear prophetic insight or the blessings of God's presence.

It is one thing to minister with spiritual gifts, but altogether another to do so in an atmosphere saturated with His parousia (manifest presence). Insisting upon utilizing our gifts to perpetuate a movement or program the Lord's presence has departed from becomes dangerous.

There are times and seasons in God. That is the pattern we discover in history. Although we constantly live under the great commission to go into the entire world and make disciples, there are times for advancement and times to withdraw to be with Him and discover His mind. Ecclesiastes acknowledges there is an appointed time for everything:

> A time to tear apart and a time to sew together;
> A time to be silent and a time to speak.
> A time to love and a time to hate;
> A time for war and a time for peace.
>   —Ecclesiastes 3:7–8

No matter how pure our motives may be, we cannot apprehend the Promised Land without the two essential ingredients Moses delineated—the Spirit's revelatory voice, represented by the leadership of Moses, and the Ark of the Covenant, which carried God's presence.

Israel's door of opportunity closed when their invitation to enter was declined. That generation was relegated to wandering in the wilderness until a new breed was birthed in the next generation. Continuing to pursue the invitation without God's blessing only ended in failure. We must be careful to follow the cloud of His presence. That was Israel's only hope, as it is ours.

Fortunately, the season of wandering has come to an end, and we find ourselves back at Kadesh Barnea. We now have another opportunity to cross the Jordan and inherit our Promised Land. But we cannot do so without learning the lessons of the past. A new form of leadership in the order of Joshua is budding. A young generation of people with hungry hearts desperate for God has been born in this day. This is the recipe for success.

We are living in a day when the Lord is re-releasing revelation of His purpose: the unstopping of old wells and the reapplication of unfilled promises. The leadership emerging today will not merely have a Church mentality but a Kingdom consciousness, that is, they do not aspire simply to bless their individual churches, but to change the spiritual atmosphere of their region.

The Kingdom perspective is to consolidate His people's faith to touch Heaven and bring His Kingdom revelation to the earth. When this is achieved, every person comes under Heaven's influence. It then becomes an individual's choice whether one gives himself or herself to this influence or not.

This is the harvest model. A general prophetic proclamation over the Body of Christ portends something fresh and new on the horizon that is as significant for the twenty-first century church as the Azusa Street revival was of the twentieth century.

IN THE ORDER OF JOSHUA

Much has been spoken and written in recent years and many have prophetically foretold the emerging Joshua Generation. The Church has now crossed a transitional threshold in Heaven's time line in apprehending this promise.

The modern Church has had difficulty adequately understanding spiritual transitions and timeliness. We have observed that most shifts of this nature develop slowly, with one season overlapping into the next. Although 2005 ended a 120-year cycle, it may take some time for this new manifestation of God's attributes to be fully revealed. Even so, it will happen.

Like Moses, Joshua had his "burning bush" experience. However, the Lord did not appear as a pillar of fire in a bush that was not consumed, but as Captain of the Lord's Host. He said:

> "...No; rather I indeed come *now* [emphasis mine] as captain of the host of the LORD." And Joshua fell on his face to the earth, and bowed down, and said to him, "What has my lord to say to his servant?"
>
> —Joshua 5:14

The Lord was with Joshua as He was with Moses, yet in a different manifestation of His nature. He came now as the mighty warrior God. So shall it be in this day. A holy militancy is about to emerge in the Bride of Christ. Many leaders will begin to surface with a Joshua anointing. Joshua means "The Lord Saves." The Joshua form of leadership will function in the Church with concise direction and profound anointing for salvation and deliverance. These leaders will be overseers commissioned to bring in a wave of harvest and entrusted with the authority and anointing to accomplish the task; they do in the last days what Paul did in the beginning: bear the message of God's Kingdom by a revelation of Jesus Christ. Paul said:

> For I neither received it from man, nor was I taught it, but I received it through a revelation of Jesus Christ.
>
> —Galatians 1:12

Great and profound mysteries of the Kingdom are about to be unveiled that will begin to displace the giants inhabiting our inheritance. Again, these insights into the divine nature and purposes will not be through the precepts of man but by the manifestation of Jesus Christ. A wonderful and rewarding season of Church history awaits.

CHAPTER

7

Where Champions are Born

T rue champions often arise from the most obscure, unexpected places—on the backside of a desert, in a field tending sheep, or drawing water from a well. For Kathryn Kuhlman, it was 4:30 on a Saturday afternoon on a dead-end street in Los Angeles; where a heart rending decision was made and a champion was born.

Kathryn Kuhlman's testimony is one in which a tremendous miracle ministry began, her personal life was transformed, and she found union with her Savior. Having experienced some measure of success as an evangelist, this specific day impacted the remainder of her life and launched her as a forerunner of the power of the age to come. On that date, according to Kuhlman, she "yielded her will to the will of the Father."

"Now, why do you cry out loudly?
Is there no king among you,
Or has your counselor perished,
That agony has gripped you like a woman in childbirth?

Writhe and labor to give birth,
Daughter of Zion,
Like a woman in childbirth;
For now you will go out of the city,
Dwell in the field,
And go to Babylon.
There you will be rescued;
There the LORD will redeem you
From the hand of your enemies."

—Micah 4:9–10

Giving birth to spiritual champions means provoking a company of people who yield themselves wholly to God so the Great Champion of Heaven can express Himself through them. Moses gave up the luxury and extravagant lifestyle of Egypt in order to bear the reproach and identity of God's people. In so doing, he initiated a spiritual principle—the more fully one surrenders in sacrificially giving oneself to the identity of Jesus, the greater the spiritual opportunity.

To the degree that we are devoted to the Lord's plans, purposes, and pursuits we will know His power and authority—to that extent. It is imperative that we understand our ultimate purpose is not to be task oriented, but relationship driven. The Lord still seeks those who will walk with Him in the cool of the day. Adam's original mandate was not merely to tend the garden but to have fellowship with God.

This generation will see great spiritual champions—"victorious ones" who know the mind of Christ and do exploits for His glory. David was one of God's foremost champions. The secret to his success was his passionate heart and single-minded pursuit of the one thing most important to him; discovering the secret place of the Most High!

MINISTERING TO GOD'S AFFECTIONS

Our call is to be Heaven's representation on earth. From among all the nations of the earth God chose Israel; and from among the Israelites God identified the tribe of Levi. From within the tribe of Levi, the sons of Zadok were awarded a special place at the Lord's table because of their loyalty and faithfulness during times of apostasy and infidelity. Ezekiel declared:

> "But the Levitical priests, the sons of Zadok, who kept
> charge of My sanctuary when the sons of Israel went
> astray from Me, shall come near to Me to minister to
> Me; and they shall stand before Me to offer Me the fat
> and the blood," declares the Lord GOD." They shall
> enter My sanctuary; they shall come near to My table to
> minister to Me and keep My charge."
> —Ezekiel 44:15–16

This reality points to the remnant, of a remnant, of a remnant. Those who sacrificially remain constant and dedicated to God and His anointing receive a specific blessing of grace and favor. When we learn to minister to the Lord, He imparts endowments of His Spirit empowering us to overcome this world's oppressions and become Heaven's representation on earth.

Many years ago my life was forever changed when I discovered that God deals with His people today in the same ways the Bible describes. That revelation set me on the course of ascertaining modern-day applications of God's Spirit working through ordinary people. For several years I devoted myself to daily study of the lives and ministries of Smith Wigglesworth, John G. Lake, Aimee Semple McPherson, Maria Woodworth Etter, William Branham, and many others. I read about the tremendous miracles, revelations, and spiritual exploits recorded in their books, sermons, and biographies, and I desired to live in the same reality of God they knew. My perspective of God's favor and blessings upon people had been strongly influenced by the ministries of healing and salvation I surveyed. While that exploration was certainly a good thing used by the Holy Spirit to awaken my spirit to personal destiny, what resulted was a single-minded pursuit of ministry, and an adjustment in my prophetic journey was required.

When the time was appropriate, the Lord took me into a spiritual experience that permanently shifted my perspective. I had been spending extended periods of time in prayer and fasting asking for ministry gifts and the ability to communicate His Word to my generation. Clearly, those are noble pursuits and ones that I continue to aspire to! However, I discovered it wasn't my highest calling.

In the experience I was taken to a courtroom in Heaven. In that place I vividly realized that Heaven's power was sufficient to grant any request. The Lord was present to hear my petition, and it was definitely clear in Heaven's courtroom that nothing is too difficult for God. Suddenly, it seemed the things I had been previously seeking were not the primary focus any longer. He was! I explicitly ascertained that my predominant calling was not to seek ministry, but to seek Him. The Lord communicated to me, "You cannot meet the needs of the people, until you have met the need of God."

The Lord has only one need—fellowship with His people. His tremendous sufferings were for that cause. The veil has been torn, and access is now granted to this generation to experience personal exchange with the Lord on a level few have ever known. It is the consummation! When we do, we will develop like the sons of Zadok the ability to "...teach My people the difference between the holy and the profane, and cause them to discern between the unclean and the clean," (Ezekiel 44:23).

JOINING WITH THE CLOUD OF CHAMPIONS

Much prayer and sacrifice has been invested in this generation; many seeds of revival and spiritual outpouring have been sown. Our legacy is as benefactors of a great spiritual inheritance and, as the Bible prophesied, reaping from vineyards we did not plant. Even so, Jesus declared, those who sow and those who reap will rejoice together. A great company of God's champions who have blazed a spiritual trail are encompassed about us! They have sown into this day as righteous testifiers and surround us, waiting for us to become heirs of our prophetic destiny. In that, we will share the Lord's victory as one body of overcomers.

In the midst of a society characterized by Babylonian confusion, a victorious band of believers will emerge who embody the virtues of those who overcome. The Bible declares that the Lord jealously desires the anointing He has placed within us (James 4:5). He is in radical pursuit of the seeds of destiny He imparted into us that will produce friendship with Him and express His life to a needy generation. You and I have been uniquely prepared to meet the demands of the generation to which we are born.

His thoughts for this phase of Church history reside within the Father's heart. The Spirit searches the depths of God's innermost being to reveal the hidden secrets of His plans and purposes and unveils them through the Spirit of Revelation.

The great prophet Moses, despite numerous failures and poor choices, is remembered as one of God's greatest champions. We discover his secret for victory in his noble prayer.

> "...if I have found favor in Your sight, let me know Your
> ways that I may know You, so that I may find favor
> in Your sight. Consider too, that this nation is Your
> people." And He said, "My presence shall go with you,
> and I will give you rest."
>
> —Exodus 33:13–14

Something fundamentally essential about knowing God's ways positions us for divine favor. We will not achieve our end-time mandate without God's supernatural blessing, intervention, and favor. God has been following in recent past a meticulous blueprint and a carefully orchestrated heavenly plan that perfectly unfolds His divine ways and documents how nothing is random in His Kingdom.

The past one hundred years manifestly illustrates a methodical release of grace and a restoration of our biblical heritage. This pattern was initiated in the days of Martin Luther and his contemporaries but escalated substantially in the last century. We are now positioned for a new release of God's grace to carry us into the next phase of Heaven's plan.

Our awesome apostolic heritage as saints is being reestablished, and this fresh move on the horizon will transform us with as much impact on the twenty-first century Church as the twentieth century champions did in their time. God's Kingdom ministry and message propels us further by "tasting the good word of God and the powers of the age to come" (Hebrews 6:5). We are being continually groomed as messengers of God's Kingdom and thus conduits of its power.

IMITATE THEIR FAITH

The Holy Spirit's directive asserted in Hebrews is to examine the faithfulness of the spiritual leaders, who have gone before us, and to observe, scrutinize, and carefully analyze their conduct and the results of their lives. We are then charged to imitate their faith, because Jesus Christ is the same yesterday, today, and forever. Hebrews 13:7–8 states:

> Remember those who led you, who spoke the word of
> God to you; and considering the result of their conduct,
> imitate their faith. Jesus Christ is the same yesterday

and today and forever.

We are not necessarily called to emulate their personal style or patterns and formulas, but rather to imitate their faith. In so doing, the Lord will do through us what He did through them with mighty expressions of power and authority.

I have had the privilege of meeting and ministering with a couple from Tacoma, Washington, who were leaders in the Latter Rain Revival of 1948 in North Battleford, Saskatchewan. What an incredible encouragement to spend time with humble and contrite vessels who provided firsthand testimony of the awesome demonstrations of God's virtue just one generation ago!

In fact, the wife was healed of barrenness in a William Branham meeting and now has three grown sons as her testimony. She testified how God's manifest presence came into the meeting, overshadowed her, and restored her female organs with a creative miracle; He granted her the promise of fruitfulness.

If we will imitate our predecessors' faith in touching God's heart to receive the anointing, we will likewise encounter Heaven and be entrusted with His virtue. A study of their lives will also help us alleviate the pitfalls and snares that caused derailment and shipwreck. This is not a time to coast but to press in all the more despite circumstances.

Many churches, ministries, and individuals have experienced spiritual transitions and restructuring in order to function more fruitfully with God's plan. The Lord is searching for saints upon whom He can place authoritative mantles of revelation and power to initiate a wave of spiritual harvest.

INVESTING IN FUTURE FULFILLMENT

The Lord has been investing in this generation's spiritual destiny for many centuries; His Spirit has been preparing for this day from the beginning. Prophets, patriarchs, and mystics of the past used their prophetic gifts to see this day and articulate its reality. As the author of Hebrews explained:

> All these died in faith, without receiving the promises,
> but having seen them and having welcomed them
> from a distance, and having confessed that they were
> strangers and exiles on the earth.
>   —Hebrews 11:13

Many saints throughout the centuries have devoted themselves to fulfilling the divine promise they saw prophetically. Hebrews 11 displays a representative collection of these champions, who discerned God's covenant pledge and surrendered themselves to it. Though they did not see its fullness in their generations, they await our apprehension of the promise so their faith, toil, and sacrifice will be fulfilled.

> And all these, having gained approval through their
> faith, did not receive what was promised, because God
> had provided something better for us, so that apart from
> us they would not be made perfect.
>   —Hebrews 11:39-40

This company of spiritual heroes and heroines is waiting upon you and me to become God's mature sons and daughters who demonstrate His Kingdom on earth so they will become perfect. They have sown into the spiritual destiny of this generation confirming what John 4 reports—those who sow and those who reap will rejoice together.

By demonstrations of faith and spiritual exploits, they obtained a testimony from God and found favor in His sight. They are a token portrayal of others throughout history who became God's friends and carriers of His heart. Though they were not allowed to experience the completion of God's promise, they invested themselves into it. The Lord has captured and harnessed all their prayers in Heaven to be released in a grand unfolding of His plan.

The Scripture states:

> Another angel came and stood at the altar, holding a golden censer; and much incense was given to him, so that he might add it to the prayers of all the saints on the golden altar which was before the throne.
>
> And the smoke of the incense, with the prayers of the saints, went up before God out of the angel's hand. Then the angel took the censer and filled it with the fire of the altar, and threw it to the earth; and there followed peals of thunder and sounds and flashes of lightning and an earthquake.
>
> —Revelation 8:3–5

Their prayers ascended before God and were captured as heavenly incense. Not one prayer has been lost. Every prayer that has ever been prayed throughout the ages to see God's promise released in the earth has been secured in Heaven and reserved for the designated day! Every prophetic prayer offered toward the harvest of the ages will be answered in its fullness. At the appropriate time, all the prayers of all saints, past and present, that have been collected on the golden altar before God's throne awaiting the fullness-of-time moment in human history—will be gathered in a censer to be mingled with fire from the altar. A specially chosen angel will then hurl the censer back to the earth in the grand, perfect unfolding of God's heavenly design. The apostle John saw this future event in his heavenly encounter and wrote of it.

We are now living in the interval identified as the harvest;

the segment of human history distinguished by Jesus in Matthew
13, where He declared that the end-of-the-age is the harvest. The
time has come for God's "victorious ones" to be birthed!

TIME IS MEASURED

In a prophetic experience I saw the Lord holding a twelve-inch
ruler in His hand. I asked what the ruler represented, and He said,
"Time—for time is measured." In the same fashion that we measure
the height and width of something with a measuring rod, so has
the Father measured out an allotment of time to accomplish His
redemptive plan. While He viewed the beginning of the measuring
rod He could also see the end. The writer of Ecclesiastes stated:

> He has made everything appropriate in its time. He
> has also set eternity in their heart, yet so that man will
> not find out the work which God has done from the
> beginning even to the end.
> —Ecclesiastes 3:11

At the same moment he contemplated Adam's creation and
earthly life, He inspected the generation ordained to live in the end-
time. While He was viewing the life of the patriarchs he was also
examining the latter-day leaders who would carry His anointing
for His grand finale. He knew the end from the beginning and
specifically imparted seeds of destiny into the hearts of a generation
to emerge at the end of time to become His champions.

Before He ever fashioned the earth He foresaw an overcoming
generation who would embody His nature and power. From this
posture of sovereignty, the Lord ordained a plan of victory and a
people of destiny.

A WOMAN OF DESTINY

John 4 records the remarkable encounter of Jesus and an individual known only as "the woman at the well." This divine rendezvous holds a profound spiritual lesson with direct application for today. John recorded that:

> There came a woman of Samaria to draw water. Jesus
> said to her, "Give Me a drink." For His disciples had
> gone away into the city to buy food.
>
> —John 4:7–8

What an incredible privilege afforded this precious woman—to be was granted a face-to-face encounter with the King of Glory! On this fateful day the Lord sent his disciples away and waited at a well for this lone lady to make her routine visit to draw water.

One can only speculate whether this exceptional woman had any inkling this day was about to be uniquely qualified as one of the most phenomenal in her life. We can only wonder if that morning seemed unusual or different when she awakened to the eastern sun. Clearly, that extraordinary day marked a point of demarcation in her life and transformed not only her but an entire city. The woman said to Him:

> "Sir, I perceive that You are a prophet. Our fathers
> worshipped in this mountain, and you people say that
> in Jerusalem is the place where men ought to worship."
>
> —John 4:19–20

As the Lord spoke to her and revealed secret information about her life, something was ignited deep within her soul. Perhaps for many years she had sought the coming Messiah and the place of worship that went beyond religious activity into a place of Spirit and Truth. Jesus told her the Father was seeking those who would do so, and He had sought her out at the well. His meat was to do the Father's will, which for this particular day included this woman's destiny. She continued:

> "...I know that Messiah is coming (He who is called
> Christ); when that One comes, He will declare all things
> to us."
>
> —John 4:25

Every day the Lord walked the earth, His journey was ordained
and specifically orchestrated by the Holy Spirit. It was the Father's
strategy to awaken the singular destiny of this woman and use
her to capture a city for God. Before the foundation of the world,
a seed of destiny was imparted into this woman that was to be
awakened in a unique fashion—by discerning the thoughts and
intentions of her heart (Hebrews 4:12). No doubt the enemy
applied all in his arsenal to destroy this woman with multiple
failures and personal defeats. Nevertheless, the Lord knew
precisely how to weave His way through all the strongholds of
doubt and rejection to awaken her spirit.

Only by seeing what is unseen can transformations of this
nature take place. On the surface, "the woman at the well" was the
epitome of shame and failure. Even so, like Kathryn Kuhlman, she
had an encounter that provoked her to "yield her will to the will
of the Father." That decision changed everything, and a champion
was born!

A PROPHETIC MODEL

The Lord has made it acutely clear to me that this encounter is a
prophetic model for the awakening of the Western Church. In many
ways, this woman's life exemplifies our condition. Metaphorically,
we have been "married" to many movements, institutions, and
spiritual programs and missed the very purpose for which we were
created. We have been espoused to denominations, associations,
and different expressions of revival and failed to join ourselves to

the One who sent us these awakenings in the first place.

The day has now arrived, however, that seeds of destiny shall be fanned into flame through the model demonstrated in John 4. The Lord could have chosen any expression of His power to capture this woman's attention; however, He simply articulated the secrets of her heart and accomplished the Father's will by awakening her to personal destiny.

The meeting at the well was not a random encounter. It was divinely orchestrated and designed to kindle a flame of destiny imparted to her before the foundation of the world. The Lord had an appointment with this woman to bring her to the awareness of her future; she received one of the greatest privileges ever bestowed upon an individual, and that same blessing will be experienced by many in this generation. We are on course for an encounter with Jesus—He is waiting for us at the well.

This prophetic paradigm will awaken the Body of Christ to her destiny! The Lord engaged the revelatory realm of Heaven to access the seed of destiny resident in this woman although covered with failure, disillusionment, and shame. It is impossible for us to become spiritual champions relying upon our own strength and virtue. Spiritual victory is the result of Heaven's impartation; of allowing the Lord to express His virtue and characteristics through an overcoming body of believers.

THE LIVING WORD

Her exclamation that she knew a Messiah would someday come to reveal the secrets of the heart and perform supernatural feats expressed the foreknown seed of destiny in her. Like the woman at the well, the Western Church, when she experiences the revelatory realm of Heaven displaying the secrets of the heart, will also awaken to supernatural faith that will win our nation. The Bible emphasizes:

> The word of God is living and active and sharper than
> any two-edged sword, and piercing as far as the division
> of soul and spirit, of both joints and marrow, and able to
> judge the thoughts and intentions of the heart. And there
> is no creature hidden from His sight, but all things are
> open and laid bare to the eyes of Him with whom we have
> to do.
>
> —Hebrews 4:12–13

The John 4 woman became an awesome evangelist because of the supernatural faith imparted to her by her experience at the well. Obviously she had previously known the sorrow of shame and failure, yet the Lord recognized a great destiny that could only have been supernaturally discerned. This woman was the Lord's choice to awaken Samaria to a day of visitation. The Bible tells us that the entire city came out to hear Christ's testimony because of this woman's word.

Our primary purpose is to identify the hidden seed of destiny inherent in this generation's champions. They presently do not have champion's appearance or résumés, but, like this little woman, they carry a seed of purpose and destiny that will be awakened to spiritual greatness.

God's Living Word reveals and discerns the hidden thoughts and intents of the heart, distinguishing between spirit and soul. All things are open and lay bare before Him; there is nothing concealed from His sight.

When manifested, it will reap the same benefits as with the Samaritan village. This woman became one of Heaven's champions because of her encounter with the Lord at the well. The Lord is the Light of the world, which when it strikes the seeds of destiny inherent in a generation, will spark them to a life of victory, and an army of champions will emerge.

The revelatory light of His end-time plan is being revealed and igniting souls to become the champions they have been ordained to be.

CROSSING OVER—THE BAPTISM OF FIRE

A baptism of fire is coming upon those who have been set apart and prepared to be mightily anointed in this juncture of Church history. The Lord clearly has a strategic blueprint with His perfect plan and purpose for this age. It is His "road map" to the Prince of Peace, with signposts along the way indicating progress. This crossroad is presently alerting us to a present release of spiritual virtue and heavenly power for vessels that have gone through a grooming and purging process to qualify them to carry this dimension of His authority.

We are now broaching the completion of a spiritual stepping-stone ultimately leading to the Lord's throne. Men and women will arise, burning with Heaven's flame ignited in their souls— embodying radical passion and extravagant devotion. Those who follow Him and experientially apprehend the baptism of fire will carry a notable deposit of heavenly virtue. These will know the reality of the prophetic proclamation spoken over the Lord Jesus by John the Baptist.

> "As for me, I baptize you with water for repentance, but He who is coming after me is mightier than I, and I am not fit to remove His sandals; He will baptize you with the Holy Spirit and fire. His winnowing fork is in His hand, and He will thoroughly clear His threshing floor; and He will gather His wheat into the barn, but He will burn up the chaff with unquenchable fire."
>
> —Matthew 3:11–12

Significant spiritual activity will surround this emerging leadership endowed with Heaven's support. Angels will ascend and descend upon God's purposes committed to this loyal group. As the Church learns to more adequately work in cooperation with God's plan, authority will be granted to release this angelic host into their function.

The anointed leadership now being commissioned has, through God's grace, captured Heaven's attention and been furnished with authority to release the heavenly host to work in consolidation with us on the earth in establishing heavenly parameters.

THREE PILLARS FOR HARVEST
The three pillars for harvest are:

Repentance—Righteousness—Power Evangelism

When we embody the Spirit of Truth, He will bring the conviction of sin that initiates godly granted repentance (John 16:8–9). The Lord promises that if we confess our sins, He is faithful and just to forgive and cleanse us (1 John 1:9).

The apostle Paul, advising his spiritual son Timothy, stated:

...in humility correcting those who are in opposition,
if God perhaps will grant them repentance, so that they
may know the truth, and that they may come to their
senses and escape the snare of the devil, having been
taken captive by him to do his will.
                              —2 Timothy 2:25–26, NKJV

Very often people mistakenly perceive needed spiritual correction with rejection. This is unfortunate and unfruitful. True correction leads to repentance that awakens us to the knowledge of the truth. It brings us to our senses and allows deliverance from devices and snares of the adversary hindering God's high call.

ESTABLISHED IN RIGHTEOUSNESS

The Lord aspires to have true righteousness emerge from an atmosphere of contrition. Right standing with God is fundamentally essential for individuals to be utilized by Him in powerful ways. Although repentance will be a vital component until the end of the age, many believers are in a passage from repentance into standards of righteousness.

The Body of Christ is presently being called to maturity. Writing to the Hebrews, the apostle admonished them to advance beyond the elementary principles into a place of spiritual adulthood. With maturity, we are poised to taste the good Word of God and the power of the Kingdom age. He challenged them and us saying:

> Therefore, leaving the elementary teaching about the Christ, let us press on to maturity, not laying again a foundation of repentance from dead works and of faith toward God, of instruction about washings and laying on of hands, and the resurrection of the dead and eternal judgment.

> And this we will do, if God permits. For in the case of those who have once been enlightened and have tasted of the heavenly gift and have been made partakers of the Holy Spirit, and have tasted the good word of God and the powers of the age to come...
>
> —Hebrews 6:1-5

Divinely granted repentance allows apprehension of a more complete knowledge of the truth. A cleansing of our soul then occurs according to the John 17:17 prayer. We are sanctified by truth and established in righteousness.

This was the principle utilized by the Lord with His early apostles. He planted His Word in their hearts and watered it with His Spirit on the Day of Pentecost. This birthed the early apostolic age in supernatural power and impartations of great spiritual authority.

TIMES OF REFRESHING
Acts 3:19 provides pivotal inspiration for transition into a posture for visitation and revival. Its exhortations is to "repent and return, so that your sins may be wiped away, in order that times of refreshing may come from the presence of the Lord."

Repentance introduces times of refreshing from the Lord's presence. This transformation opens the door for the establishment of righteousness and the anointing for harvest as Peter demonstrated in the days following Pentecost.

Recent outpourings of God's Spirit, including the one at Brownsville Assembly of God beginning in 1995, inaugurated a specific heavenly strategy by stressing repentance. We have recently experienced a season of transition into a more pronounced emphasis on believer's righteousness. Many messages will ensue from God's leaders highlighting intimacy with Jesus and close fellowship with His Spirit. These messages will forge our nature and character according to His.

FRIENDS OF GOD
There is a holy longing birthed in the souls of many to enter into a place friendship with God promoting spiritual refinement. That is the spiritual secret to the lives of those remembered in the Hebrews 11 "hall of fame." The Lord has many servants, but very few friends. The truest form of friendship calls for the removal of all masks and veils. That has been part of the emphasis of the "angels that gather" that work with the Holy Spirit to equip us.

We presently have an unprecedented opportunity to join the company identified as the "friends of God." To them, profound secrets and Kingdom mysteries will be confided (John 15:15).

Righteousness is best described as sharing the Lord's divine nature and escaping the world's corruption and its lusts (2 Peter 1:4). Being endowed with Christ's nature allows us to reflect His image. Then we can be entrusted with awesome deposits of heavenly virtue and authority without corrupting their purity.

Experiential apprehension of these foundations will impart God's enablement for us to complete the third stage—power evangelism. True spiritual harvest is the integration of the Word and Spirit producing a demonstration of God's Kingdom and power.

We can discover our perfect example in Christ's ministry. The Bible records that He went about Judea teaching in their synagogues, declaring the message of the Kingdom and healing all manner of sickness and disease (Matthew 4:23). He supplied the purest definition of power evangelism.

END-TIME MANDATES

Our present times are both sobering and exciting. End-time mandates and promises are positioned to be released to a body of people prepared for them. A yielded cooperation with the Holy Spirit is necessary for our preparation. Even so, many Christians are undergoing a marked increase in intensity and focus related to this grooming process.

The Spirit of the Lord is placing His finger on life issues He desires to extract. As we sincerely repent of these shortcomings, a grace is released to cleanse us and prepare us in righteousness. True repentance is not the mere recital of empty words, but an expression of godly sorrow for sin. When the Lord sees His image reflected in us, then there will be notable releases of His power essential in the great harvest.

CHAPTER

8

The Shining Ones

Amazing Grace, how sweet the sound,
that saved a wretch like me.
I once was lost but now am found,
was blind, but now I see.

The Lord has promised good to me,
His word my hope secures.
He will my shield and portion be,
as long as life endures.

When we've been here ten thousand years
bright shining as the sun.
We've no less days to sing God's praise,
then when we've first begun.

Bright shining as the sun! John Newton's "Amazing Grace" is one of the most beloved Christian hymns. I wonder if he fully understood a portion of the lyrics containing a prophetic decree that will find its fulfillment in this generation—a people "bright shining as the sun."

"Angels that gather" are sent from the Lord to help prepare end-of-the-age saints by extracting from His Kingdom everything contrary to His nature. The Bible tells us that the Kingdom on Heaven is within us. The righteous will shine like the sun in our Father's Kingdom when the tares and stumbling blocks have been extracted from our soul. Light dispels the darkness of our soul as He lights the candle of our innermost being. Jesus prophesied what will follow that refining work:

> "THE RIGHTEOUS WILL SHINE FORTH AS THE SUN in the kingdom of their Father. He who has ears, let him hear."
> —Matthew 13:43

Jesus affirmed that sons of God's Kingdom will be on earth that shine like the sun. His desire is to establish His nature and character in all who have ears to hear. The message coming forth requires revelatory anointing to fully comprehend it. A significant aspect of His plan is to incite a body of people to be so saturated with Him that they are illuminated with the "Son's" brightness.

When Moses descended from Mount Sinai holding the two tablets of the Testimony, he did not know that the skin on his face "shone while he talked with Him." Prophetic end-time messengers empowered with God's grace to encounter Him will shine as bright lights in dark places. This company of believers will be uniquely prepared, equipped, and commissioned for this specific time in human history to radiate with the brightness of a burning torch (Isaiah 62:1).

THE STANDARD OF DANIEL
Daniel was a fascinating prophet on many levels. His strength of

character and personal devotion undoubtedly captured Heaven's attention. He became a spokesman to his generation and ours, as well as a prophetic model for today's leadership and the generation he foresaw.

His life typifies the maturation of many leaders in this end-time generation. Like this notable prophet, men and women of high esteem, who will not yield to the fear of man, are poised to emerge. True representatives of God's Kingdom always maintain a reverence and awe of God that overrides the fear and manipulation of men.

As with Daniel and his three friends, many emerging leaders have discovered the Lord in the "fiery furnace" and the "lions' den" and surfaced as overcomers. The Lord is about to speak profoundly, and the time has arrived to hear what He will tell us:

> ..."O Daniel, man of high esteem, understand the words
> that I am about to tell you and stand upright, for I have
> now been sent to you." And when he had spoken this
> word to me, I stood up trembling.
>
> —Daniel 10:11

As in Daniel's day, many of God's people have been residing in spiritual Babylon. Great confusion has permeated the Christian faith. Regardless, we await God's promised restoration to a perfect standard; in fact, this process has already been set in motion and greatly advanced during the Latter Rain outpouring and continues today. The plumb line, by which all truth will be measured, is in the Lord's hand. Zechariah prophesied spiritual restoration saying:

> For who has despised the day of small things? But
> these seven will be glad when they see the plumb line
> in the hand of Zerubbabel—these are the eyes of the

Lord which range to and fro throughout the earth.
—Zechariah 4:10

Spiritual restoration can only be produced by the written Word being mightily anointed by the Sevenfold Spirit of God to accentuate the treasures of wisdom and knowledge hidden in Christ. This consolidation produces the full revelation of Jesus Christ to be delivered to the end-time generation by those who eat the now unsealed book brought by the hands of a strong angel.

This mysterious book is first found in Daniel 12:3–4 as the prophet was instructed concerning the end-time generation. He foretold that:

> Those who have insight will shine brightly like the brightness of the expanse of heaven, and those who lead the many to righteousness, like the stars forever and ever. But as for you, Daniel, conceal these words and *seal up the book* [emphasis mine] until the end of time; many will go back and forth, and knowledge will increase.

Our prophetic directive guides us to arise and shine brightly during days of great darkness. We have the scriptural assurance that this wonderful promise spoken to Daniel for those living in the end-of-time era must be fulfilled. Secrets and spiritual mysteries essential in making this a living reality will be discovered in this incredible book of destiny. Many will go "back and forth" to apprehend its truth and delegate to this generation what has previously been preserved as hidden manna.

Understanding this paradigm is essential in implementing God's plan for the harvest. It will mark the empowerment of a company of people who will be given authority as overseers to reap the first wave of harvest. Schools of ministry will teach this revelatory insight and God's army will be ignited with the illumination of His glory.

Wonderful disclosures of Daniel 12:4 are now being revealed. The Lord is offering the Bride His open book. We are not merely to read it, but to eat it so that it becomes a part of our constitution. That instruction was given to John, and so also is it for us. To merely recite this revelatory truth does not suffice; we must exemplify it. We are meant to become living epistles of end-time truth.

IN THE FATHER'S RIGHT HAND

We first discover this book as it is sealed in Daniel's day. We find it next in the Father's right hand, as He sits upon His throne of ultimate power and authority in the book of Revelation. It had been preserved in Heaven to keep the revelation a secret from humanity and our adversary.

> I saw in the right hand of Him who sat on the throne
> a book written inside and on the back, sealed up with
> seven seals. And I saw a strong angel proclaiming with
> a loud voice, "Who is worthy to open the book and to
> break its seals?"
>
> —Revelation 5:1–2

If the mysteries of God's consummation had been discovered at an inappropriate time, then humankind would clearly have perverted them as we have most all of our inheritance throughout history. If our enemy realized this book's contents, he would aspire to counterfeit them as he has virtually everything God has delegated to us. This book was preserved by the Father until Someone was found worthy to take it from His hand and reveal it at the appointed time.

Only the Lord Jesus overcame and qualified to take the book and break its seals. What an incredible day we live in! So great was

His act that all Heaven worshipped the Lord for His worthiness. The four living creatures and the twenty-four elders fell on their faces before the Lord in this magnificent prophetic fulfillment.

He opened the book of redemption and the full revelation of who He is. The mysteries of God's Kingdom are delayed no longer! Many patriarchs and prophets throughout history longed to understand what will be freely given to this generation of overcomers.

Apprehending the truth contained in this veiled book will illumine us with the brightness of His presence and the strength of great understanding. Then we will lead many to righteousness in a great harvest of souls. It pleases the Lord for us to embody His light. When we lead life as those who are "native-born" to the light, we enjoy the fruit or effect of that light—kindness, uprightness of heart, and truth. This light will manifest as the Sevenfold Spirit of God in the same way that pure white light directed through a prism highlights the seven colors of the spectrum.

This generation's saints will walk in the revelatory light they possess. Our walk with the Lord must be experiential both tangibly and practically so that we exude the spiritual light deposited in us.

Following this model will draw the lost to the Kingdom of Light; it will attract those walking in darkness to our light and fulfill the prophecies of Daniel, "Those who have insight will shine brightly like the brightness of the expanse of heaven, and those who lead the many to righteousness like the stars forever and ever."

A NEW SONG

This book is a key to the harvest. The song sung in Heaven at the breaking of its seals emphasizes its role in the great harvest and the calling of many to righteousness. The four living creatures and the twenty-four elders sang:

..."Worthy are You to take the book and to break its
seals; for You were slain, and purchased for God with
Your blood men from every tribe and tongue and people
and nation. You have made them to be a kingdom and
priests to our God; and they will reign upon the earth."
                                            —Revelation 5:9–10

Daniel stressed that the words of this book were to be concealed
and reserved for the latter-day generation. He was specifically
told to, "...*conceal these words and seal up the book until the end of
time*" (Daniel 12:4). We are there! As the seals are broken Heaven's
host acknowledges the Lamb's great sacrifice and the relationship
between the unveiling of this book and the harvest of souls
purchased with His blood.

The revelation, interpretation, and application of Kingdom
truth contained in this book emphasizing the full measure of
power, wisdom, might, and glory to be revealed—will convey
those virtues and be disclosed to all mankind.

THE STRONG ANGEL

The opened book is next discovered in the hand of a strong angel
descending from Heaven. He has a rainbow around His head and
feet like pillars of fire that He places on the land and sea (Revelation
10:1–7). Who is this strong angel? He can be none other than the
Angel of the Covenant who led Israel as a pillar of fire by night and
cloud by day. He now brings the complete revelation of the Lord's
covenant to present the bridal company without spot or wrinkle.
He is introduced to Israel in this way:

"Behold, I am going to send an angel before you to
guard you along the way and to bring you into the
place which I have prepared. Be on your guard before
him and obey his voice; do not be rebellious toward

him, for he will not pardon your transgression, since My
name is in him.

But if you truly obey his voice and do all that I say, then
I will be an enemy to your enemies and an adversary
to your adversaries...But you shall serve the Lord your
God, and He will bless your bread and your water; and I
will remove sickness from your midst."
                                                —Exodus 23:20–23, 25

This Angel represented God's manifest presence among
His people. The Spirit of the Lord visited this nation with an
expression of His presence during the last generation. The Latter
Rain outpouring was much more than just a healing revival; it was
the sowing of seeds for the great harvest. More notable things were
accomplished than most presently comprehend. Great end-time
pledges were set in motion. Marked understanding involving the
mysterious book concealed by Daniel was inaugurated; yet to the
twenty-first century generation, the strong angel returns with the
now open book in His hand and offers it to be consumed.

The attributes displayed by the strong angel speak
prophetically of the characteristics of God's glory to be
experienced in this unfolding.

Clothed with a cloud—A token of His presence, power, and
   leadership
A rainbow upon His head—A symbol of covenant
His face shining like the sun—The glory of God in the
   face of Christ
Feet like pillars of fire—His parousia coming to earth
In His hand is the opened book—The revelation of the
   book of redemption

**He steps on the earth with His right foot on the sea and
His left on the land**—To Israel and the Bride
He cries out with a loud voice, like the roar of a lion—The
shout of ultimate victory

PASSING OF THE TORCH

The prophetic events of the Latter Rain Revival carried far more
impact than most realize. The strong angel was introduced in
that previous generation through a "Moses" anointing that
brought people out of captivity. Thousands witnessed undeniable
spiritual events never before seen in Church history. Many of
those occurrences have been mentioned in my books. William
Branham, Roland Buck, and others were used by God's Spirit to
release deposits of great spiritual value we will come to know in
their fullness.

Although many people have difficulty with the last few
years of William Branham's life, much of which resulted from
misunderstanding and miscommunication, the supernatural
nature marking his ministry is well documented, in which a
divine presence operated on a level that had not been seen since
the early Church. Not only was God's manifest presence visibly
experienced by thousands—many of whom I have personally
interviewed—but also photographed. My objective here is not to
validate any individual's ministry but to uncover what the Lord is
telling this generation.

Never before had a man stood before God's people on a
consistent basis and revealed detailed thoughts and intentions of
their hearts as a mode ministry. That was the same pattern Jesus
used with the woman at the well; only the Lord fully working
through a yielded vessel could produce such fruit.

Even Branham's worst critics acknowledge that the
manifestation of God's Spirit he elicited transcended anything
previously known and was strikingly accurate. My question is,

"What does this mean for us? What was the Holy Spirit pointing to?" While I enjoy reading these wonderful testimonies, I am more interested in understanding the implications of this phenomenon for our day. Was it another carefully orchestrated step in God's perfect plan for the ages?

I believe, at least in part, that Branham's ministry was intended to direct us to end-time portions of God's Word in preparation for truly stupendous divine acts of revelation and power. We are going to be the beneficiaries of the greatest grace ever demonstrated to a generation—a capstone generation emerging with shouts of "Grace, grace"—and bring in an exceptional harvest to the Lord.

The strong angel will reengage this generation with a Joshua anointing to carry people into the covenant of the open book. Though the Lord walked with Joshua as He did with Moses, His presence with Joshua conveyed an entirely different aspect of His virtue. He reappears now with the opened book in His hand so its revelations can be prophesied to the nations. If the "calling out" of the prior generation came with great power, then how much more will we see in the "crossing over" generation?

We are promised the manifestation of His presence as He beckons those who overcome to take the opened book and not merely read it but devour it. When we do, we will see the Scriptures in an entirely new light. Our understanding of His Word will increase substantially while seemingly veiled passages, scarcely understood, will be clearly illumined.

God's Kingdom mysteries will be made evident. This book's revelations entail *becoming* something more than *doing* something; becoming God's mature sons and daughters—the Word made flesh once again. Then we will do all that is ordained for this day.

THE OPEN BOOK CONCEALED AND REVEALED

The open book will be offered to those who are hungry for His presence and are passionate to know Him as fully as He may be known. The bridal calling woos us to consume and assimilate it by the consolidation of Word and Spirit. Then anointed teachers and wise counselors will shine with the brilliance of the sun and reap a harvest, turning many back to a place of right standing with God.

FOUR REVELATIONS OF THE BOOK

1. Mysterious revelations entrusted to Daniel and sealed until the end-time (Daniel 12:4)
2. Held by the Father until the Worthy One prevailed to open the book (Revelation 5:1–2)
3. The strong angel descends from Heaven with the now opened book containing God's mysteries for a calling out (Revelation 10:1–7)
4. The strong angel offers the opened book to the end-time company who will consume it and prophesy to the nations for the harvest of the ages and the crossing over (Revelation 10:8–10)

Simply to intellectually analyze the truth of the open book with theological dissertations and religious jargon would grossly undersell its importance. Its truth must be mingled with the Spirit of Revelation to give it life and substance, which, when we have fully experienced this, will have formed Christ in us and promoted spiritual maturity. The Lord's desire is to completely redeem and sanctify our spirit, soul, and body by preserving us whole and without blame at His coming.

Now may the God of peace Himself sanctify you entirely; and may your spirit and soul and body be preserved complete, without blame at the coming of our Lord Jesus Christ.

—1 Thessalonians 5:23

The supernatural element in this destiny cannot be denied. As with Paul, these mysteries will unfold by the revelation of Jesus Christ (Galatians 1:12). Although the open book will be sweet in our mouths, it will become bitter in our stomachs. We will not be satisfied just to absorb this book; we must also prophesy its revelation to many nations, peoples, and kingdoms. Into that day we have now transitioned!

HOW DO WE ACCESS THE BOOK?

John was told, "Go, take the book which is open in the hand of the angel who stands on the sea and on the land... and eat it" (Revelation 10:8–9). What does it mean to eat the open book? That is a question I consistently asked many years ago when the Lord first began dealing with me concerning this passage. I discovered the answer when the Spirit of Revelation fell upon me and I experienced a biblical truth firsthand.

As Christians we conceptually embrace the reality of the Lord's crucifixion. We read the gospel accounts and intellectually accept the validity and authenticity of God's word. By faith, we wholeheartedly welcome the Lord's advent two thousand years ago as Emmanuel and His surrender of Himself to be butchered at the hands of His own creation.

However, when the revelatory anointing came upon me that morning, I was taken in the spirit and allowed to see the Lord's suffering on the cross. That changed my perspective eternally! No longer was this an historical fact I believed; I experienced it as a living panorama that deeply ingrained itself in my spiritual DNA; a scene now woven into the very core of my existence. That is what it means to eat the open book.

The prophet Ezekiel experienced these qualities in his generation. He was not simply allowed to articulate prophetic words to Israel; he had to become a living expression of them. The Lord demanded he:

> "...eat this scroll, and go, speak to the house of Israel."
> So I opened my mouth, and He fed me this scroll. He
> said to me, "Son of man, feed your stomach and fill
> your body with this scroll which I am giving you." Then
> I ate it, and it was sweet as honey in my mouth.
> —Ezekiel 3:1–3

After the prophetic words were entrusted to Ezekiel, the Holy Spirit came upon him to make them experiential. He was taken by the Spirit to see a living expression of the prophetic utterance he was directed to deliver.

> Then the Spirit lifted me up, and I heard a great
> rumbling sound behind me, "Blessed be the glory of the
> LORD in His place." And I heard the sound of the wings
> of the living beings touching one another and the sound
> of the wheels beside them, even a great rumbling sound.
> So the Spirit lifted me up and took me away; and I went
> embittered in the rage of my spirit, and the hand of the
> LORD was strong on me.
> —Ezekiel 3:12–14

The Lord is able to cause His Word to be filled with Spirit and Life to such an extent that we are willing to die for it. Paul beseeched the Lord for that impartation when he prayed we would be filled with the Spirit of Wisdom and Revelation so we may know Him experientially with an all-consuming knowledge. Such access helps us better understand the hope of our calling and sacred destiny in Him, the riches of the glory of our inheritance, and the surpassing greatness of His power extended to believers (Ephesians 1:17-19).

TO WALK WITH GOD

People are becoming increasingly fascinated with the biblical patriarch Enoch. Spiritual seeds of destiny are being awakened that provoke us beyond theological reflections into a place of intimate relationship—where we "walk with God." Many are finding themselves identifying with Enoch's life and his friendship with the Lord. Genesis 5:21–22 records:

> Enoch lived sixty-five years, and became the father
> of Methuselah. Then Enoch walked with God three
> hundred years after he became the father of Methuselah,
> and he had other sons and daughters.

After Methuselah was born, then Enoch walked with God. What transpired at Methuselah's birth? A line of demarcation was drawn in Enoch's life that marked the remainder of his days on earth. He had an experience that was so significant it influenced the balance of his life.

We can ascertain a portion of that secret in the naming of his son. In ancient times the naming of a child directly signified aspects of the child's personality and destiny. Biblical scholars claim the most accurate meaning of Methuselah is "When He Is Dead, It Shall Be Sent."

Historically, we know at the time of Methuselah's death, the world was changed forever by what is known as Noah's flood. Enoch saw something experientially and named his son accordingly. More importantly, Enoch walked with God on an intimate level few have ever achieved following this revelation.

What transpired at Methuselah's birth became such a part of Enoch's core existence that for the remainder of his life, Enoch enjoyed intimate friendship and profound revelatory experiences with God. His life is an example of those who eat the open book and experience the revelation of Jesus Christ. The remaining days of their lives will be marked by open Heaven experiences and revelatory encounters that bring God's Word to life.

THE HEAVENS OPENED

The New Testament gospels depict intense angelic activity surrounding the Lord Jesus' ministry. Jesus stated His disciples would see the Heavens opened and angels ascending and descending upon Him (John 1:51), a prophetic proclamation that directly correlated His life and ministry with Jacob's experience at Bethel. In Genesis, God revealed Himself to Abraham, Isaac, and Jacob as El Shaddai. In each case, a specific divine attribute essential for the patriarchs to become fruitful, multiply, and occupy the land of their sojourning was imparted. Genesis 28 outlines Jacob's experience:

> Then Jacob departed from Beersheba and went toward Haran. He came to a certain place and spent the night there, because the sun had set; and he took one of the stones of the place and put it under his head, and lay down in that place.

> He had a dream, and behold, a ladder was set on the earth with its top reaching to heaven; and behold, the angels of God were ascending and descending on it.
> —Genesis 28:10–12

God's wonderful blessing delegated to Abraham was no ordinary blessing, but one assuring to accomplish for him and his son and grandson what they could not do for themselves in achieving their destiny and fulfilling God's promise. Immediately following the release of this blessing upon Jacob, he was subsequently granted an open Heaven experience that unveiled his own divine destiny and his people's.

That evening Jacob lay down to sleep on a rock and immediately experienced the supernatural. The blessings created a gate for the Heavens to open allowing Jacob to see a spiritual ladder joining Heaven with earth and a host of angels ascending and descending. He testified, "What an awesome place this is! It is none other than the house of God, the very gateway to heaven!" (Genesis 28:16, NLT).

Jacob saw the Lord standing at the head of the ladder representing Himself as El Shaddai. And one encounter with El Shaddai utterly ruined Jacob for life. No longer could he live as a supplanter or deceiver but was transformed into Israel, a prince submitted to God. This feature of God's nature is directly associated with divine destiny and apprehending the open book.

Jacob received a spiritual impartation from Isaac through which he experienced the Heavens opened and divine access he had not previously known. He called it the very gate of Heaven and the house of God.

Jesus personalized that experience in telling Nathaniel Heaven would open and angels would ascend and descend upon Him, not just upon a place. The Lord is our ultimate example. Our prayer is for the Heavens to open above us so angels may ascend and descend upon the end-time generation to do greater works and allow us to consume the revelation of Jesus through spiritual blessings and impartations from the Holy Spirit.

Presently, the Holy Spirit is preparing many within the Body of Christ to encounter the Lord in such a way that heavenly objectives are revealed and imparted. Issuing out of that place we become fruitful and multiply and begin to occupy the land of our sojourning.

UNDERSTANDING THE BLESSING

While at a prophetic conference in Dallas, I shared God's divine attributes as El Shaddai. I taught on the different definitions I had learned in scholarly books to help articulate this representation of God's nature. I communicated how the Lord will present Himself as the "All Sufficient One" and the One who is "more than enough."

At the end of the message a Hebrew professor approached me. He was a very kind man and spoke favorably of the message I had just delivered. However, he kindly asked if he might broaden my understanding of God's nature as El Shaddai. Naturally, I recognized I was about to receive a lesson in Hebrew—a much needed one. He advised me that what I had shared about God as El Shaddai was accurate but incomplete—not the pure interpretation of this name—and related the many facets of the Hebrew language that more fully illustrated this nuance of God's virtue. He declared that a simple definition would be, "He is the God of utter ruin and devastations who is able to do for us what we cannot do for ourselves."

The biblical order in which God revealed His infinite nature through His names is significant. Each time He described Himself with a different name He communicated an important lesson and unveiled fresh dimensions of His plan for humankind. El Shaddai is the eighth name God attributed to Himself. The number eight indicates a time of new beginnings.

God appears to Abraham in Genesis 17 after He promised a son to Abraham and Sarah. Once their bodies were impotent and incapable of fulfilling their promise by natural means, God revealed Himself as El Shaddai. He accomplished what Abraham could not attain in his natural strength.

The present-day application of this truth is significant. We have strived to attain God's promises corporately and individually. Once we have exhausted all natural means, then God Almighty, El Shaddai, appears in tangible form and intervenes, doing for us what we cannot do for ourselves. Thus He gets all the Glory. Personal encounters with Jesus will "ruin" us regarding the spirit of this world and render us desperate to know Him more.

The Lord's blessing will open the Heavens for us as He did for Jacob, which will grant access to the revelatory realm and make His Word living and experiential. Then we do not merely have a prophetic word for this generation—we become the living word.

CLOAKED WITH LIGHT

He is the light of the world, and we are to reflect that marvelous light. David described the Lord saying, "...Covering [Himself] with light as with a cloak, Stretching out Heaven like a tent curtain" (Psalm 104:2).

The Lord clothes Himself in light as with a virtuous garment to depict His great authority in Heaven and in creation. We are similarly called to be endowed with the raiment of light that proceeds from Him. We are called to be the light and the salt of the earth.

Heaven's pure white light will proceed from the throne and be imparted into the spirit and soul of believers to make us divine carriers of His virtue. Many will encounter the lights of Heaven in private worship and in corporate settings in amplified ways over the coming months and years.

> He made the moon for the seasons;
> The sun knows the place of its setting.
>
> —Psalm 104:19

The Church is often represented by the moon, reflecting the light of the sun and marking Heaven's times and seasons. Our call is to reflect His great light. We are now approaching the time in which the light of the moon will be as the light of the sun (Son), and the sun will be seven times brighter—like the light of seven days. Isaiah prophesied:

> On every lofty mountain and on every high hill there will be streams running with water on the day of the great slaughter, when the towers fall. The light of the moon will be as the light of the sun, and the light of the sun will be seven times brighter, like the light of seven days, on the day the LORD binds up the fracture of His people and heals the bruise He has inflicted.
> —Isaiah 30:25-26

The Lord promises to share His power and authority through overcoming believers identified as His bride. Only by His presence resting in them can the bride fulfill her prophetic destiny and reap the harvest of the ages. The Church's prophetic voice is intended to announce to the world Heaven's appointed times and seasons and God's activities on earth. As we press in to the revelatory realm of Heaven, we will gain a deeper understanding of this important role.

The Lord's voice is as the sound of thunder. He will speak with far greater clarity in the coming days to those with "ears to hear." He stands at the door knocking, His revelatory voice hearkening to the people anointed with the Spirit of Wisdom and Revelation to welcome Him and minister to Him in their priestly role.

CHAPTER

9

Engaging Heaven

A. W. Tozer was one of the twentieth century's most prolific teachers. His epitaph simply and appropriately reads, "A Man of God." He developed an intimate relationship with the Lord that transformed him from an uneducated farm boy into a revelatory mouthpiece to his generation and ours. He once declared, "A true prophet is one who knows his times and what God is trying to say to the people of his times."

The Lord's Spirit delivers clear revelation that is strategic for our time and fully addresses our present condition in order to awaken us to personal and corporate destiny. Delegated to each generation is a Kingdom message that penetrates into the souls of those prepared to receive it. The word of truth proceeding from God's heart is directly related to the spiritual circumstance of the hour. To be relevant in our generation, we must present "meat in due season" that the Holy Spirit deems appropriate.

Each of the seven Churches of Asia Minor received diverse corrections, admonitions, and rewards based on their spiritual atmosphere. Much of our ability to receive God's heart depends on our moral and spiritual condition as well as the relevant social considerations of the times. Now is not the time for mechanical and repetitious articulation of doctrines and precepts that have little or no pertinence to this generation's needs. Our call is to "come up here" and apprehend God's blueprint.

Many ministries teach the prophetic Scriptures. However, our greatest need is for prophetic messages of God's Kingdom to address our spiritual climate and launch us into our prescribed destiny. We do not merely need to teach about prophecy but to be prophetic believers. The times necessitate scholarly presentations of our spiritual past, as well as revelatory insight for the future so we know where we are presently positioned in Heaven's economy.

A KINGDOM PORTRAIT

The journey into God's Kingdom starts with our spiritual birth and involves much more than going to Heaven after death. The Lord's desire is to exemplify His great victory and appropriate the power of His blood through a body of people on this side of eternity. They will be known as "sons of the Kingdom," who work cohesively with His Spirit to function as kings and priests.

When the time came for Joshua to distribute the land of promise among Israel's tribes, the tribe of Levi received none of the land. Instead, the Lord made the simple yet enormously profound statement, "I am your portion and your inheritance among the Israelites." Who can measure in land or monetary value the riches of this truth? Nevertheless, that is precisely the promise to the new covenant royal priesthood—those who have Him have everything. Such a great mystery will find fulfillment in this present time. The Holy Spirit promised to:

> ...bring to light what is the administration of
> the mystery which for ages has been hidden in
> God who created all things; so that the manifold

wisdom of God might now be made known through
the church to the rulers and the authorities in the
heavenly places.

                                        —Ephesians 3:9–10

Throughout Church age dispensations, the Lord has been
emphasizing incremental revelations involving the cooperation
between Heaven and earth in the fulfillment of end-time
mandates. The earlier days constituted the sowing of spiritual
seeds; now is the appointed season for the harvest of all seeds.
These days will mark the maturity of all that has been sown,
both good and evil.

To achieve our highest purpose in God requires divine access
to the Spirit's supernatural realm. God's Word emphatically
proves this inevitability, especially the book of Acts, where
apostolic seeds were sown. Apart from the Holy Spirit, mankind
is incapable of acquiring one of His greatest gifts—the ache of
a burning heart towards God. Before we can be translated into
God's high calling, we must first feel consuming spiritual hunger
reminiscent of the first century champions.

Someone once asserted that Esau's fatal flaw was moral
complacency, while Jacob's only virtue was his bitter
discontentment. Even so, Jacob was the one the Lord highlighted
as harbinger of His promise and facilitator of His plan, because
resident in Jacob's heart lay a desperation for God's blessings,
although his methods were less than commendable. Nevertheless,
an unseen virtue hidden in Jacob's soul captured the Lord's
attention and distinguished him from his brother Esau.

A clear distinction and separation is taking place within God's
people. Heart motivation is the primary dividing line. As Jacob
was differentiated from Esau, so will a similar severing take place
within the Body of Christ. Both were sons of Isaac, but Jacob was
motivated by a different spirit. Jacob's years of service to Laban

sifted unrighteousness from his soul and provided preparation for his name to be changed from Jacob (supplanter) to Israel (a prince with God). God's people are being asked, "Whose Kingdom will you build?"

RECOGNIZING THE TRUE ENEMY

It is an important spiritual mandate to have enlightened eyes to see where we are presently placed in human history and the unfolding of God's redemptive plan. Equally important are gifted eyes that can foresee our prophetic destination. From this perspective we can set our sights on the goal of our faith, as well as recognizing the snares and traps of the enemy intended to hinder our ability to get there.

Jesus vowed to extract all stumbling blocks from His Kingdom and everything contrary to His nature, along with those that commit lawlessness. The end of the age will be marked by a separation between those who serve God and those who do not. This delineation has also been prophesied by Malachi. We are presently living in the day of its fulfillment.

> Then those who feared the LORD spoke to one another, and the LORD gave attention and heard it, and a book of remembrance was written before Him for those who fear the LORD and who esteem His name. "They will be Mine," says the LORD of hosts, "on the day that I prepare My own possession, and I will spare them as a man spares his own son who serves him." So you will again distinguish between the righteous and the wicked, between one who serves God and one who does not serve Him.
> —Malachi 3:16–18

Satan once boasted, "I will make myself like the Most High"

(Isaiah 14:14). Through religious activity and human reasoning our adversary effectively emulates the working of God's Spirit in ways appealing to the human soul. Such may seem right in the eyes of mankind, but the end result is destruction. God's Spirit and the antichrist spirit have worked concurrently throughout Church history to a place of maturity now requiring separation.

The Lord's Spirit has been speaking very pointedly to His people concerning these ancient spiritual enemies that infiltrated the early Church, which are in the process of maturing to harvest. Children of Light are beckoned to a place of adulthood in order to engage these adversaries. A portion of the gathering angels' assignment is to co-labor with us in this duty. The Lord is pressing us "...to restore the land, to make them inherit the desolate heritages" (Isaiah 49:8).

The first-century Church fathers recognized that the greatest battle was internal more than external. Jude, believed by many to be the Lord's brother, pinpointed the magnitude of this conflict in his epistle. He admonished the believers of his day, and ours, to contend earnestly for the faith that was once and for all delivered to the saints. That battle was within the Body and involved false leaders anointed with corruptive counterfeit spirits. He said:

> For certain persons have crept in unnoticed, those who were long beforehand marked out for this condemnation, ungodly persons who turn the grace of our God into licentiousness and deny our only Master and Lord, Jesus Christ.

> Woe to them! For they have gone the way of Cain, and for pay they have rushed headlong into the error of Balaam, and perished in the rebellion of Korah.
>
> —Jude 1:4, 11

He identified certain spirits that work to undermine the foundations of faith and direct God's people away from the source of their salvation.

The spirit of Cain—A religious spirit leading to jealousy
   and murder
The spirit of Balaam—Merchandising the anointing for
   unrighteous gain and false teaching
The spirit of Korah—Rebellion against God's appointed
   leadership

Our confrontation is not with flesh and blood but with spiritual forces usurping a position of dominion in heavenly places. The battle will be won in the spiritual realm—liberating people held hostage by prisons of intimidation, manipulation, and control.

It is reasonably easy to diagnose the blatant perversion, deadly unbelief, and unlawful spiritism permeating this present age. The more difficult confrontation, however, lies within the Church—with false spirits masquerading as authentic spiritual authority. By developing discernment and examining spiritual fruit, a distinction can be noted as we approach maturity.

> But solid food is for the mature, who because of practice
> have their senses trained to discern good and evil.
> —Hebrews 5:14

High on the Holy Spirit's agenda is His desire to deal with these influences that separate people from the walk of intimacy the Lord so emphatically yearns for.

IDENTIFYING STUMBLING BLOCKS

One such spirit is identified as the spirit of the Nicolaitans. Early apostolic leaders discerned this spirit raising its evil head during the first-century Ephesian Church Age.

The Lord commended the Church fathers, through His friend John, by saying, "Yet this you do have, that you hate the deeds of the Nicolaitans, which I also hate" (Revelation 2:6). The early Church did not tolerate this diabolical spiritual influence and we must not either.

Some commentators previously believed this term denoted a group of misguided disciples under the influence of a man named Nicholas—some truth to this argument is possible—nonetheless, credible historical evidence concurring with this position is difficult to find. Instead, this newly introduced spiritual nemesis quite likely constituted a counterfeit spirit so detrimental to God's purposes that He acknowledged hatred of it, for it represented a perverted form of leadership whose objective contradicts the Holy Spirit's motive. The Lord's Spirit will always draw people to the Lord Jesus, while counterfeit spirits will seek to lead people away from the Lord and His life-changing presence.

Paul warned of this danger:

> Be on guard for yourselves and for all the flock,
> among which the Holy Spirit has made you overseers,
> to shepherd the church of God which He purchased
> with His own blood. I know that after my departure
> savage wolves will come in among you, not sparing the
> flock; and from among your own selves men will arise,
> speaking perverse things, to draw away the disciples
> after them.
>
> —Acts 20:28–30

Ravenous wolves have but one objective—to devour sheep. Paul vividly portrayed a common cultural staple to highlight the importance of recognizing this foe and its violent nature. He noted this spirit's motive was to draw disciples after themselves, rather than pointing them to the Lord Jesus.

The "deeds of the Nicolaitans" constituted a movement initiating the rise of a priestly hierarchy ultimately usurping the place of Christ Jesus over the people. For this reason Jesus abhors it: It separates Him from His people. The Lord once informed me, "You cannot meet the needs of the people until you have first met the need of God."

The only need He has is to fellowship with His people. Anything obstructing that relationship engenders His wrath. He is not looking for a slave-bride as a concubine, but a covenant marriage typified by Sarah, Abraham's wife, for through Sarah the child of the promise was conceived.

NICOLAITAN SPIRIT DEFINED

The Nicolaitan spirit will masquerade as a true spiritual administration wielding counterfeit spiritual authority by subtly using fear, manipulation, and control to achieve its agenda. The term Nicolaitan is derived from two Greek words— *Nikos* and *Laos*.

Nikos is defined as conquest; victory; triumph; to conquer; and, by implication, dominancy over the defeated. The word *nicao* literally means to dominate, intimidate, and manipulate. *Laos* simply means "the people" or the "laity." Together the phrase signifies "to conquer (dominate-intimidate-manipulate) the people (laity).

The Lord applauded the Ephesian Church for opposing the Nicolaitans. However, over the following generations this spirit grew in its power and influence. By the fourth-century Pergamum Church Age, the Lord departed from commending the Church for not tolerating this spirit to condemning the Body for their appeasement. The latter membership wasn't fully convinced of the poisonous problem posed by this spirit and tolerated its existence within the Church.

> 'But I have a few things against you, because you have
> there some who hold the teaching of Balaam, who kept
> teaching Balak to put a stumbling block before the sons
> of Israel, to eat things sacrificed to idols and to commit
> acts of immorality. So you also have some who in the
> same way hold the teaching of the Nicolaitans.'
>   —Revelation 2:14–15

Balaam was an Old Testament prophet who taught the king of Moab the rebellious strategy inciting God's discipline by inducing Israel to sin through intermarriage with the idolatrous Moabites. The intermarriage problem continued throughout Israel's history until it finally reached its apex many years after Balaam introduced it, when King Ahab finally married Jezebel, the idolatrous daughter of Ethbaal, priest-king of the Zidonians. This union produced an unrighteous leadership in Israel that compromised their standards as God's covenant people (1 Kings 16:31).

When the adversary was unsuccessful in cursing God's chosen people, he altered his approach. What he could not perpetrate by direct confrontation he easily accomplished through stumbling blocks and snares facilitated through compromise. Though Balaam was unable to curse Israel, his teaching eventually led God to judge Israel by convincing her to violate her covenant with God by intermingling with Balak and his idolatrous followers.

The "way of Balaam" is the covetous conduct of "hirelings," whose primary motive is to commercialize their divine gift. The "teaching of Balaam" is the promotion of a mercenary ministry counseling the Body of Christ to abandon godly separation and noble character in favor of worldly conformity. Paul wrote about this conflict:

See to it that no one takes you captive through
philosophy and empty deception, according to
the tradition of men, according to the elementary
principles of the world, rather than according to Christ.
—Colossians 2:8

Our adversary has disseminated numerous false teachings throughout Church history, including the doctrine of cessation. This detrimental belief held that spiritual gifts, signs and wonders, and the working of miracles described in the New Testament all ceased to be applicable to the contemporary Church. Even today, numerous theologians teach that supernatural signs, wonders and healing discontinued in the ministry of the Church with the end of the apostolic age and the closing of the canon of Scripture.

Thankfully, the Holy Spirit is highlighting that what Jesus Christ has performed in prior generations He will continue to accomplish today. Like our early apostolic fathers, we will know the God of power and experience personal encounters with Him to transform us and our generation.

When we walk in faithful communion with God, He delegates impartations of anointing and authority to us that our enemy cannot overcome. The adversary's strategy for victory is to corrupt God's people by seduction with the spirit of this world. Spiritual compromise always results in wrong relationships; concession inevitably precedes a premature demise, while loyalty to God and His Word facilitates repentance, restoration, and victory.

GODLY ADMINISTRATION
Clearly, the Lord intends to empower appropriate Church government to equip His people for service. Without leadership or the administration of godly authority, lawlessness and confusion reign. True apostolic leaders convey the spirit of godly authority

by presenting messages of truth that usher God's people into His presence and mobilize them to do the work of ministry.

A careful examination of Church history readily demonstrates how the Nicolaitan movement launched the beginning of an unrighteous priesthood. Again, our intent is solely to identify spiritual influences that have successfully stolen the saints' inheritance throughout the Church ages so we will be more aptly positioned to overcome as Christ overcame and thus be seated with Him on His throne.

In Matthew 13 Jesus identified tares as "sons of the evil one." This company functions by an antichrist spirit and possesses awesome power that appeals to the human soul—mind, will, and emotions—rather than by God's Spirit. The term *antichrist* is often considered to mean "against Christ"; the more complete definition would be "another Christ." The spirit Paul called the "working of iniquity" is actually another gospel vying to substitute for the true gospel.

God's Spirit is provoking "sons of the Kingdom" to mature, so this counterfeit spirit can be discerned more fully and exposed. Witchcraft, sorcery, and control spirits motivated through worldly wisdom will emerge with blatant audacity and power in this age. The "sons of the Kingdom" must likewise mature to the place of "tasting the good Word of God and the power of the age to come" and release the reality of Christ in us, the hope of glory.

This is the spiritual inheritance symbolically described as the "land beyond the Jordan" as we cross over into the day of promise. Illumination will be coming to those who formerly embraced traditionalism and religious structures, and many will embrace His divine light. The apostle Paul referred to this issue in Colossians 2:23:

> These are matters which have, to be sure, the appearance of wisdom in self-made religion and self-abasement and

severe treatment of the body, but are of no value against fleshly indulgence.

Leadership's guidance and oversight of a New Testament Church should not need manipulation or a control spirit to function; in fact, these directly contradict the Holy Spirit's standard. People will follow character and the recognition of God's favor. Leaders are called to lead by example—to model Christ-likeness. Control, intimidation, and political spirits are neither needed nor welcome.

OVERCOMING THE NICOLAITAN SPIRIT

The first item on the Nicolaitan spirit's agenda is to divide and conquer. The primary objective of this spirit is to separate the Body from the Lord's provision for leadership, including the insight of genuine spiritual authority. Normally, this is accomplished by accusing and persecuting biblically based leadership established by the Holy Spirit.

This form of opposition promotes distinguishing people into two classes—the priest and the laity. This philosophy will advocate an "us and them" perspective within the Church. Further, there is no mention in the New Covenant Word where priests or ministers mediate between God and the people, nor where they are separated in their worship of the Lord.

The proper scriptural view is that the Body of Christ is a diverse people, each having different gifts from God, yet all members indispensable to the well-being of the entire spiritual body. Also, no hierarchy is supposed to exist in the Body of Christ—all are called to minister together as one body headed by Christ. God desires all to love and serve Him together, though some may have different functions than others.

The Nicolaitan spirit destroys those precepts and separates the ministers from the people, rendering the leaders overlords instead of servants. The Lord expressed His hatred for this type of administration and expected His people to do likewise. In other words, there are to be no intimidating, controlling, power-hungry officers in the Church exercising counterfeit authority over the "laypeople."

Believers who are genuinely filled with the Holy Spirit and in radical pursuit of the Lord openly embrace godly leadership, counsel, and direction as a platform for growth and a safety net against demonic snares. There is an obvious need for definite leadership in every generation. The primary objective in this outline is to identify prevailing attributes of spiritual influences that distinguish true from false. The Bible admonishes us to grow in maturity by exercising our senses to discern good from evil.

The Scriptures plainly support a priesthood of believers, each being granted access to the Father through the Son.

> You are A CHOSEN RACE, A royal PRIESTHOOD,
> A HOLY NATION, A PEOPLE FOR God's OWN
> POSSESSION, so that you may proclaim the excellencies
> of Him who has called you out of darkness into His
> marvelous light...
> —1 Peter 2:9

As in the days of Elijah, a confrontation with the prophets of Baal is imminent. The Nicolaitan spirit will be challenged in this hour. The early Church, beginning with the Ephesian Church Age, confronted this form of opposition following the outpouring of the Holy Spirit on the Day of Pentecost.

> Children, it is the last hour; and just as you heard that
> antichrist is coming, even now many antichrists [anti-
> anointed, emphasis mine] have appeared; from this we

know that it is the last hour.

—I John 2:18

FIRST LOVE AFFECTION

The spirit of the Nicolaitans will target Christians who have lost their "first love." This enemy will meticulously orchestrate events intended to quench fiery passion for things of the Spirit. His design is to impart spiritual indifference and a heartsick disposition from deferred hope. The admonition to return to her first love, given to the Ephesian Church Age, is also the predominant message in overcoming this adversary in our generation. The spirit of the Nicolaitans will always be accompanied by apathy and lethargy. These will cool our affections toward the Lord and the passion with which we are to carry out His purposes.

When we remain constant in the simplicity and purity of devotion to Jesus, we will then clearly discern and distinguish the unholy attributes of the Nicolaitan spirit and the righteous qualities of Spirit appointed leadership. The Nicolaitan spirit deteriorates the structure of the Church body by attempting to create subordinates rather than brothers and sisters. Slaves brought under this kind of authority are always distraught and nervous because of the great responsibility and expectations to please their masters. This creates an irrational spirit or a neurotic mind-set rather than a spirit of peace, promoting insecurity rather than abiding strength.

Currently, a large segment of Christians who have come under the influence of this evil spirit are oppressed with a variety of nervous conditions, hopelessness, and discontentment and leave Churches because of the wounds that result and their feelings of insufficiency. The good news is that God is about to sift out this spirit and cause a distinction between His Spirit and the counterfeit that has flourished throughout the Church Ages.

Spirit appointed apostolic government will be marked by such attributes as servanthood, humility, and righteousness after

Jesus' unblemished example, and its leaders will have power to demonstrate the end-time message. They will convey the message and ministry of God's Kingdom.

False leadership will attempt to set itself above genuine godly anointing and usurp a position in the Church rightfully belonging to the Holy Spirit. The Church is not a democracy— government by the people or rule of the majority; but a Theocracy—government by immediate divine guidance or by officials regarded as divinely guided.

A. W. Tozer recognized the need for this delineation in his mid-twentieth century ministry:

> "If Christianity is to receive rejuvenation it must be by other means than any now being used. If the Church in the second half of this century is to recover from the injuries she suffered in the first half, there must appear a new type of preacher. The proper, ruler-of-the- synagogue type will never do. Neither will the priestly type of man who carries out his duties, takes his pay and asks no questions, nor the smooth-talking pastoral type who knows how to make the Christian religion acceptable to everyone. All these have been tried and found wanting."

Tozer went on to prophesy:

> "Another kind of religious leader must arise among us. He must be of the old prophet type, a man who has seen visions of God and has heard a voice from the Throne. When he comes (and I pray God there will be not one but many) he will stand in flat contradiction to everything our smirking, smooth civilization holds dear. He will contradict, denounce and protest in the

name of God and will earn the hatred and opposition of a large segment of Christendom. Such a man is likely to be lean, rugged, blunt-spoken and a little bit angry with the world. He will love Christ and the souls of men to the point of willingness to die for the glory of the one and the salvation of the other. But he will fear nothing that breathes with mortal breath."

THE MIGHTY COUNSELOR

When the Lord was teaching me about this struggle, I had a revelatory experience that vividly portrayed our calling to confront this spirit. The Holy Spirit took me to a sanctuary filled with Christians. It was a traditional church setting with a choir loft, wooden pews, and several hundred well-dressed followers. It was as though I were in the service and standing adjacent to the podium but unseen by anyone present. The people were attentively listening to one of the most articulate preachers I have ever heard. He was incredibly handsome, with a very dark complexion, dark hair combed directly back, and a custom-made three-piece suit. I was amazed at his command of the English language and the methodical delivery of his message.

Everything seemed appealing, but I felt unrest in my soul. His words seemed almost true yet contained some form of leaven that twisted the truth in almost unnoticeable ways. On the surface what I was witnessing appeared appropriate but the spirit behind it was unsettling.

To my right, I saw in the spirit a man with white hair and beard approaching wearing a white robe. He appeared ancient yet young and vibrant at the same time. He walked directly adjacent to me and inquired what I thought of the meeting.

I told him that everything seemed good and acceptable but my spirit was also disturbed. He said, "Why don't you apply the blood of Jesus to the meeting?" I responded that the service was well attended, the people were focused on the messenger, and the message was almost correct. "Why should I apply the blood to the meeting?" I asked.

He replied, "If this man is from God, applying the blood of Jesus will only amplify what he is doing; if he is not, it will tear it down." I asked who I was speaking with; He said his name was the Mighty Counselor. I immediately remembered Isaiah's prophecy concerning the Messiah and the divine attributes he would embody. I later discovered that the Hebrew word translated as "wonderful" in most English versions of the Bible had multiple expressions that capture the full meaning of the term.

> For a child will be born to us, a son will be given to us;
> And the government will rest on His shoulders;
> And His name will be called Wonderful Counselor,
> Mighty God, Eternal Father, Prince of Peace.
> —Isaiah 9:6

With that I heeded His counsel and applied the blood of Jesus to the meeting. When I did, there was an immediate reaction in the service and particularly with the minister. Instantly, his thoughts seemed to be broken and his disposition shaken. I did it again, and the reaction was only increased. I continued to apply the blood of Jesus until the messenger's demeanor expressed total disarray.

Suddenly, in my experience, the preacher vanished from my sight although I could still hear from him a barrage of verbal threats and accusations against me that were staggering. More than ever before, I understood how the victory at the cross disarmed vain philosophy, deception, and false authority. Paul emphasized this in his letter to the Colossians:

> See to it that no one takes you captive through

philosophy and empty deception, according to the
tradition of men, according to the elementary principles
of the world, rather than according to Christ.
For in Him all the fullness of Deity dwells in bodily
form, and in Him you have been made complete, and
He is the head over all rule and authority... When He
had disarmed the rulers and authorities, He made a
public display of them, having triumphed over them
through Him.

—Colossians 2:8–10, 15

I realized I was witnessing how our adversary has infiltrated churches with a false anointing that is so close to the genuine that it would deceive the very elect if possible. Personal ambition and human agendas are the leaven that can distort our revelatory clarity. Our earnest prayer should be for the deliverance of our own perspectives in order to embrace His. Only from such a posture can we fully apprehend the heavenly model to be emulated on earth.

Spiritual discernment is being conveyed to this generation to no longer tolerate lukewarm Christianity nor empty church services void of the Lord's presence. This is a hungry generation that must know the Lord experientially; only the Lord will satisfy their desperation.

Our perfect pattern is the Lord Jesus Himself. The Father still seeks pure and unbridled obedience. Much of what is to come has not even entered into the hearts of humankind. Therefore the Spirit of Revelation is essential for it to be birthed. We will do what we see Him doing and say only what we have heard in the heavenly realm.

RESTORING OUR AFFECTIONS

Impartation from Heaven's supernatural authority makes one

an apostle according to biblical standards. The New Testament contains numerous warnings against false leaders drawing the flock astray with counterfeit authority. The Nicolaitan spirit will not appear as an enemy; rather veiled as righteous leadership promoting seemingly appropriate agendas.

The Scriptures make it plain; God has never placed His Church in the hands of an elected leadership that moves with political mindedness. He has placed His Church in the care of God-ordained, Spirit-filled, Word-living men and women who lead the people with meekness and faithfulness—shepherds who willingly lay down their lives for the sheep and will only feed them the Spirit-breathed revelation of the Word.

The winds of change are blowing. The Church must now comprehend the vast distinction between the impartation of spiritual gifts and the delegation of spiritual authority. Many in the Body of Christ have the mistaken notion that their dynamic spiritual gifts qualify them to be recognized as apostolic leadership; nonetheless simply possessing powerful gifting alone does not meet the biblical qualification of apostleship.

God's government appropriately placed in the Body of Christ to ignite the flame of passion for fellowship and union with the Lord, will be:

1. Chosen by Him
2. Ordained by Him
3. Equipped by Him
4. Sent by Him

> While they were ministering to the Lord and fasting, the Holy Spirit said, "Set apart for Me Barnabas and Saul for the work to which I have called them." Then, when they had fasted and prayed and laid their hands on them, they sent

them away.

—Acts 13:2–3

God appointed leadership endowed with the apostolic authority modeled by the first-century Church will fulfill these same biblical mandates. The Lord's commissioning and delegation of spiritual authority, along with the impartation of mighty gifts of the Spirit are what warrant true leadership. Miracles, signs, and wonders will always characterize this company. These endowments are essential in order to pull down principalities and powers within churches or geographic regions and establish a spiritual foothold for the Kingdom of Heaven.

They will:

1. Function as spiritual fathers and mothers fulfilling the prophetic directive of Malachi 4:6, to restore the hearts of the children to their fathers and the hearts of the fathers to their children.

2. They will enjoy the blessing of El Shaddai to be fruitful, multiply, and occupy the land of our sojourning. This is the model for expansion and growth.

3. The Lord is our judge, lawgiver, and King (Isaiah 33:22). These three divine offices held by the Lord represent His design for appropriate governmental structure. This government is a spiritual administration, but likewise reflects the three offices our nation has recognized. We have the judicial, legislative, and executive branches of our government. All spiritual government was exemplified by the Lord and is to be embodied by His people.

4. Their relationship with the Lord will be experiential. Paul's apostolic commission included his privilege to see the Lord and hear utterances from His lips (Acts 22:14). This is the birthing of apostolic ministry according to early Church standards.

5. They will be witnesses or testifiers of the Lord's resurrection. Our Messiah is the only One who was raised from the dead as proof of His divinity. There must be a validation of that reality in our generation. A true witness can only testify of what he or she has seen and heard (1 John 1:3).

6. They will be carriers of resurrection power. This company will taste the good Word of God and the powers of the coming age as a validation of their commission (Hebrews 6:5).

THE HAND POINTS THE WAY

We are entering a very dangerous season in Church and human history. We must be very careful about the object of our focus—is it the Kingdom of Heaven or the spirit of this world? Have we devoted our attention to God's desire or to pursuing our own ambition? These pressing questions must be truthfully confronted! We cannot afford distractions from the adversary; distractions can lead to destruction.

To fully achieve our mandate, God's spiritual government must function with authority. We are living in a day when miracles, signs, and wonders are an essential component of our New Testament heritage. As with the early Church, God's healing power and extraordinary exploits provide divine validation necessary to meet mankind's great needs and establish His governmental order.

Used wrongly, God's power can also disqualify our

participation in His plan and do great damage. History has glaringly attested to how the careless handling of God's power results in shipwreck. This is a sobering reminder of our serious need for integrity and personal character. God will not share His glory with another. Our ministries must be galvanized with charity and cloaked in humility.

Biblically based five-fold leadership will always do all in their power to point believers to the Lord and encourage them to cultivate deep and passionate roots with the Lord Himself. Their greatest desire will be to see others equal and even surpass the spiritual standards they themselves enjoy. The spiritual gifts and authority assigned to them will be diligently implemented with one objective—to espouse the people to Jesus.

In every age, God's spiritual voice validated by signs and wonders always calls that generation back to the Lordship of Christ. This was especially true during the Latter Rain Revival as numerous ministers admonished the Body of Christ to relinquish their personal agendas and programs to embrace intimate relationship with the Holy Spirit.

Moses had a face-to-face friendship with the Lord. That exchange fostered God's desire for complete leadership of His covenant people. When we in this generation discover that place of friendship, we will also perceive more fully how the spirit of antichrist has infiltrated the Church with a counterfeit anointing that usurps the Spirit's leadership.

IN THE ORDER OF ELEAZAR

Eleazar was Abraham's faithful servant. He was entrusted with the oversight and stewardship of Abraham's household. When the time came for a wife to be found for Isaac, Abraham assigned significant gifts to Eleazar to win the attention of Isaac's bride. True leadership will have the heart of Eleazar. He openly acknowledged the gifts were not to draw Rebekah to him, but to the one that sent him.

As my friend Bobby Conner often says, "It is the height of tyranny to take the gifts God gave us to woo the bride to Jesus, and instead draw them to us." The heart of true leadership will always guide the people to the One who sent them, not allure them away. Properly maintaining this alignment has been a constant battle throughout history. The prophets of Israel encountered similar deceptions.

Jeremiah addressed the spiritual fathers of his day and rebuked them for leading the people away from true worship into the snares of human reasoning.

> An appalling and horrible thing
> Has happened in the land:
> The prophets prophesy falsely,
> And the priests rule on their own authority;
> And my people love it so!
> But what will you do at the end of it?
>   —Jeremiah 5:30–31

> For my people have committed two evils:
> They have forsaken Me,
> The fountain of living waters,
> To hew for themselves cisterns,
> Broken cisterns
> That can hold no water.
>   —Jeremiah 2:13

Considerable authority is about to be imparted to many believers throughout the Body of Christ. We have a choice to make! Are we going to use these gifts and spiritual endowments to draw the people to the Lord or to build our own ministries, typified by the cisterns outlined in Jeremiah's prophecy?

Resolving this issue in our hearts beforehand, will help qualify us for leadership! When the Lord appeared to Solomon and granted his wise request, the answer was already hidden in Solomon's heart. Before his day of visitation came, Solomon had purposed in his soul to ask for a good thing—a hearing heart that discerns God's perfect will. When the wise petition was heard, God said to Solomon:

> "Because you had this in mind, and did not ask for
> riches, wealth or honor, or the life of those who hate
> you, nor have you even asked for long life, but you have
> asked for yourself wisdom and knowledge that you
> may rule My people over whom I have made you king,
> wisdom and honor have been granted to you..."
>   —2 Chronicles 1:11-12

The Lord is aching to initiate unity and fraternal affection between the various members of His body. Overly focusing on the enemy's exploits will tend to distract and divide us. Likewise, if we unduly focus on leaders as spiritual icons we may lapse into perversion. These snares will be destroyed when we adhere to the mandate to return to our first love and rivet our gaze solely upon the Lord. In so doing, righteous leadership will be recognized in its proper balance and harmony.

This army will then be unleashed to oppose the deeds and doctrines of the Nicolaitan spirit's venture to steal the believer's birthright. This will catalyze the Body of Christ to step into position to do the work of ministry, since the ultimate call of God's government is to equip and prepare the Lord's Body for activation. This army's attributes will unequivocally display true godly leadership. The Bible plainly portrays genuine leadership in the Church as well as distinguishing it from those identified as false. The plumb line of this ministry will be its fruit. Our calling is to maintain a thorough recognition of the fruit generated through genuine apostolic leadership so as not to be deceived by the false.

The spiritual adversary described in the book of Revelation as the Nicolaitans ventures to overshadow God's aspiration to release total liberty among believers and mobilize His people into a royal priesthood. That trend will change as we grow more adept at discerning His presence and walking more intimately with Him.

10

The Full Measure of His Reward

The Moravian community in Herrnhut, Germany first initiated their round-the-clock prayer watch in 1727 and continued nonstop for the next one hundred years. Eventually, this fellowship of faithful believers commissioned thousands of missionaries around the world. Their dedication and success in sowing the seeds of God's Kingdom is well documented; some even sold themselves into slavery in order to win the slaves. The fruit of their labor is ongoing and the influence of their devotion continues to burn brightly.

John Wesley was one of the many spiritual leaders of the eighteenth century experiencing spiritual transformation through the Moravians. He recorded in his personal journal that while on a voyage across the Atlantic to become a missionary in America, his life was forever altered during a fierce storm that threatened the safety of the ship. While he and others were gripped with fear, he noticed a humble group of Moravians totally at peace and even joyful in the midst of the storm.

He then realized they had a salvation in God he had not

experienced. This turning point launched one of the greatest voices of God's Kingdom since the Great Reformation. Wesley discovered the truth that we are saved by God's unmerited favor, through faith in Him; not by our own works and striving.

The Moravians captured a portion of God's heart involving the harvest, one that we must also embrace. A 1791 evangelical report highlights this reality saying:

> "The simple motive of the brethren for sending missionaries to distant nations was and is an ardent desire to promote the salvation of their fellow men, by making known to them the gospel of our Savior Jesus Christ. It grieved them to hear of so many thousands and millions of the human race sitting in darkness and groaning beneath the yoke of sin and the tyranny of Satan; and remembering the glorious promises given in the Word of God, that the heathen also should be the reward of the sufferings and death of Jesus; and considering His commandment to His followers, to go into all the world and preach the gospel to every creature, they were filled with confident hopes that if they went forth in obedience unto, and believing in His word, their labor would not be in vain in the Lord. They were not dismayed in reflecting on the smallness of their means and abilities, and that they hardly knew their way to the heathen whose salvation they so ardently longed for, nor by the prospect of enduring hardships of every kind and even perhaps the loss of their lives in the attempt. Yet their love to their Savior and their fellow sinners, for whom He shed His blood, far outweighed all these considerations. They went forth in the strength of their God and He has wrought wonders in their behalf."

WORTHY IS THE LAMB

The Moravians' rallying cry was, "May the Lamb that was slain receive the full reward of His sufferings." The essence of all that we do in our ministry is centered on this truth that is also emphasized in Revelation 5:9–10:

> And they sang a new song, saying, "Worthy are You to take the book and to break its seals; for You were slain, and purchased for God with Your blood men from every tribe and tongue and people and nation. You have made them to be a kingdom and priests to our God; and they will reign upon the earth."

Our earnest longing is for Jesus to receive the full measure of His reward. Mel Gibson's, *The Passion of Christ*, graphically depicted the Lord's sufferings. He willingly endured the cross in order to purchase for God, men and women from every nation on earth.

The message of the Cross is incredibly powerful; providing mankind with grace to experience the redemption of their souls, to such a degree, that God delegates His Kingdom authority to us. The Bible plainly illustrates the Lord's desire to make us priests and kings before God; a place of great responsibility requiring spiritual maturity.

This generation's calling is to advance into spiritual adulthood in order to demonstrate the Lord's Kingdom on earth. The bridal company's assignment is to follow His example and demonstrate the "greater works." The fullness of His Kingdom will not be realized until His return. Nevertheless, God's Word promises that we will taste that realm on this side of that notable event. The mandate for this generation's overcoming Christians is to prepare the Lord's people for His return; those working to this end are considered "friends of the Bridegroom."

All generations of saints have prayed to see Heaven's Kingdom revealed on earth. The saints of old contended for Christ's inheritance, that He might receive the fullness of His reward. He purchased for God, men and women from every nation on earth— referring to the gentile age. The diverse nations of the earth denote all who will embrace Christ before the emphasis of God's plan is returned to Israel and the Jewish people. The fullness of this reality is yet to be completed; nevertheless, it will transpire before the end of the gentile age.

The Moravian's often recited noble prayer, clearly defines the bridal company's heart motivation—the Lord Jesus receiving a reward worthy of His sacrifice. It is not about angels or demons or us as individuals, nor even spiritual experiences, although all are incorporated in seeing that He receives the fullness of His sacrifice. Our ultimate purpose is to experience union with Jesus and cooperate with His Spirit to see the wealth of His sacrifice recognized in this generation and His harvest realized.

This truth will form our cornerstone in the last-day outpouring. There is an escalation of release on earth to facilitate His Kingdom's revelation so that Jesus receives His complete reward. Highlighted revelatory truth is being set before us through words, not taught by human wisdom but by the Holy Spirit; consolidating spiritual truth with spiritual language through those possessing the Spirit of Understanding. There are corporate and personal messages proceeding from God's heart relative to our destiny and position in Heaven's economy. Paul said:

> Now we have received, not the spirit of the world, but
> the Spirit who is from God, so that we may know the
> things freely given to us by God, which things we also
> speak, not in words taught by human wisdom, but in
> those taught by the Spirit, combining spiritual thoughts

with spiritual words.

—1 Corinthians 2:12–13

Gaining the understanding that the Lord is grooming us for something significant transforms our mind-set and generates hope to displace hopelessness. Without this comprehension we would indeed experience profound hopelessness and despair. A double portion restoration and recovery of lost heritage is our legacy. The Lord is opening our eyes and ears with the Spirit of Understanding so our discernment is taken to greater levels to accomplish this purpose.

Our souls have been sifted—establishing contrition, humility, and meekness—so that we may carry greater levels of power and authority. Deep spiritual understanding illumines this reality and mobilizes God's people for this great task. As Paul taught, the Spirit of Wisdom and Revelation gives individuals understanding of our rich inheritance in Christ.

The Lord is granting the Spirit of Revelation to open "eyes and ears" to a place of fellowship with Him that displaces despair and depression. In its place, "first-love" affections are being re-ignited. Holy desperation is saturating the hearts of a bridal company who will not be satisfied merely hearing the testimony of others who have encountered the Lord Jesus—they must have their own experiential relationship.

There is a clear admonition in John 10:27, "My sheep hear My voice, and I know them, and they follow me." We are promised the ability to experientially apprehend the undeniable perception of His voice. The more acutely familiar we are with His voice, the more capable we become of recognizing the counterfeit.

There has been a carefully orchestrated adversarial plot to invalidate this aspect of our heritage. The desolate heritage of the saints is being restored. The progressive restoration promised in Joel 2:25 is presently taking place. Heaven's doors are being opened, granting unprecedented access to the Spirit's realm, and fellowship with Heaven. The Lord prophetically outlined this privilege when He said:

> "To him the doorkeeper opens, and the sheep hear his voice, and he calls his own sheep by name and leads them out."
>
> —John 10:3

The Lord is calling us by name and leading us out of the dungeons of bondage and oppression into a place of freedom and liberty—where the Spirit of the Lord is, there is emancipation. An overcoming army is emerging, and the invitation is being issued to enter a place of fellowship with the Lord that equips us for this long foretold confrontation. Neither the Nicolaitan spirit nor other adversaries can continue to hold the Bride of Christ hostage, who is destined to be joined with the Lord in a promised union.

FINDING HIM

The Lord assures us that those who seek Him will find Him. There is a present emphasis on this direct spiritual invitation. Jeremiah prophesied that:

> "Then you will call upon Me and come and pray to Me, and I will listen to you. You will seek Me and find Me when you search for Me with all your heart."
>
> —Jeremiah 29:12–13

The Father is seeking those who will worship Him in Spirit and Truth. We think we are seeking Him, but in reality, He is pursuing us. Thank the Lord for that! That reality is highlighted in the Lord's continuing pursuit of His Bride and our response to Him.

The wisdom expressed through a seeking heart will function

as a key that unlocks Heaven's resources and grants access to God's power, glory, and authority. The Spirit's intervention and enablement is essential in our quest to know the Lord intimately and do exploits to His glory.

HE CHOSE US

Many Christians perceive themselves as explorers seeking God, but more appropriately, it is God seeking us. We did not choose Him but He has chosen us. Moreover, He is desperate for us to transcend simply living as servants and cultivate a forum for friendship with Him expressed in the adoration of Mary.

> But the Lord answered and said to her, "Martha, Martha, you are worried and bothered about so many things; but only one thing is necessary, for Mary has chosen the good part, which shall not be taken away from her."
>
> —Luke 10:41–42

Perhaps each of us has a little of Mary's and Martha's attributes resident within us.

The Martha mentality is motivated more by the human soul—mind, will, and emotions—while Mary is moved by the spirit. Martha is a servant but Mary discovered friendship with the Lord.

Both mind-sets are essential but must be maintained in proper order. Our purest service to Him is motivated from a place of friendship and the revelation of His desire we obtain by waiting admiringly upon Him. The Lord is more concerned about what we are *becoming* than what we are *doing*. Both are important, however, our greatest gains are accomplished in the Spirit after we are fashioned in His image and bear His nature.

To each is given a measure of faith; even the faith by which we acquire spiritual blessings is God's gift. Our prayer is for a great awakening to occur involving our incredible destiny that mobilizes and launches many believers into friendship with the Lord and fruitfulness in His Kingdom.

MOVING INTO MATURITY

The Lord is presently speaking very pointedly about the Church's need to move into spiritual maturity. Many people living in this generation have a unique and holy attribute woven into their spiritual DNA. A predetermined virtue provokes us to move beyond the outer court and into the Holy Place and the expression of His Kingdom—it is divine destiny.

Our adversary has worked diligently to release the "spirit of stupor" over the Western Church. This diabolical scenario blinds our eyes and shields our ears to spiritual truth, promoting a sense of satisfaction to simply live in a justified state without being incited to greater depths in God. The Lord has saved us *and* He has given us a holy calling—a divine destiny. The Scripture declares that He:

> ...has saved us and called us with a holy calling, not according to our works, but according to His own purpose and grace which was given to us in Christ Jesus before time began...
> —2 Timothy 1:9, NKJV

God's covenant people have a function and responsibility while living in this world. If we become content to simply remain in the elementary principles of the faith, we may never achieve the notable destiny and holy calling prescribed for our lives. With spiritual maturity, we can be entrusted with tremendous virtue and authority necessary to impact our generation with the Kingdom's message—we were born for this objective.

These blueprints for our lives are already recorded in Heaven's archives (Psalm 139:16). It remains up to each of us individually to cooperate with the Lord in their fulfillment.

CONFORMED TO HIS IMAGE

Our ultimate personal destiny is to be conformed to the image of Jesus Christ. We are not certain what we will be like in the conclusion of time, but we know that we will be like Him because we will have seen Him as He is. What an incredible assurance! 1 John 3:2 outlines this promise saying:

> Beloved, now we are children of God, and it has not appeared as yet what we will be. We know that when He appears, we will be like Him, because we will see Him just as He is.

The Lord is indicating His desire to restore through His people the original mandate for mankind, and fully heal the breach existing since man's fall in the garden. Our churches, cities, and regions will then reflect Heaven's light to the degree the saints within them do.

The Lord is granting believers eyes to see and ears to hear the revelation of divine destiny. This realization breaks the spirit of despair and hopelessness. It launches us into an inheritance set aside for us before the foundation of the world. This grace was purchased at a great cost—the blood of Jesus Christ. We are the "joy" that was set before the Lord for which He willingly endured the cross, although He despised its shame.

Much truth is presently being spoken about the provision for our destiny. This trend will escalate in the days ahead. One of the foremost aspects of identifying our destiny is to also understand the stewardship of spiritual provision essential for its fulfillment.

The Lord is drawing a "line in the sand" as a boundary or

line of demarcation to determine who will cross over and wholly submit themselves—spirit, soul, and body. We are presently living at a crucial juncture in time that will be looked upon for years to come as a pivotal crossroad in human history. We must carefully make our choices and decisions through prayer and greater understanding of His Word.

UNDERSTANDING OUR CALLING

Scripture teaches that gaining spiritual understanding provides a valuable tool to preserve and sustain us in our earthly journey. The quest for divine understanding is an expedition for treasures of greater value than gold and silver. With spiritual insight we are able to extract every nugget of wisdom and possibility for advancement allowed by the Holy Spirit.

One of the greatest achievements one can attain is to comprehend our calling and access the allotted provision for it. We have a holy calling and function in God's grand design. Furthermore, we have a spiritual inheritance essential for its realization.

> ...In Him also we have obtained an inheritance, having been predestined according to His purpose who works all things after the counsel of His will...
> —Ephesians 1:10–11

The Spirit of Revelation takes us into God's heart where treasures of wisdom and knowledge are safeguarded. There we discover our pre-ordained designed destiny initiated before the world was fashioned. These were established after the counsel of His will to accomplish His purposes on earth. The ones who acquire this wisdom discover the great prize of His high calling.

We have been saved by grace but in addition to our salvation, we are assigned a function in God's Kingdom. The Bible symbolically describes us as living stones fitted into place in the construction of a holy temple. Each stone is vital to the overall integrity and effectiveness of the structure. Very often the stones are tested and tried before being placed into their rightful position. In the end, God is glorified and we share in His reward.

TESTING OF RIGHTEOUSNESS

We have now crossed a threshold to do what we have for so long talked about. This is especially true in the Western Church. This is the day of Lights or the day that people begin to walk in the Light of Heaven. The patriarch Job once conveyed this longing:

> "Oh that I were as in months gone by,
> As in the days when God watched over me;
> When His lamp shone over my head,
> And by His light I walked through darkness;
> As I was in the prime of my days,
> When the friendship of God was over my tent."
>   —Job 29:2–4

Job expressed the desire of many in this generation—that the Lord's lamp of divine favor will shine over us. By that "light" we fruitfully walk through this dark generation and enjoy friendship with God. This positions us with priestly garments necessary for our call to minister to Him in the beauty of holiness.

There could be many purposes outlined for the testing of Job's righteousness. Clearly, one of the Lord's designs in this endeavor was to bring Job to a place of heightened relationship and authority as His earthly representative.

> "Now gird up your loins like a man,
> And I will ask you, and you instruct Me!"
>   —Job 38:3

In this divine encounter, Job was permitted to see the Lord and clearly discover his own deficiency. This further allowed him to be girded more completely with the Lord's strength. He concluded:

"I have heard of You by the hearing of the ear,
But now my eye sees You.
Therefore I abhor myself,
And repent in dust and ashes."
                                        —Job 42:5–6, NKJV

Job's testing ultimately catapulted him to a higher plain and sphere of authority before God. He could then be trusted with greater levels of intimate relationship as the Lord's intermediary on earth; that was his high calling and divine destiny.

The Lord has always had a witness on earth to declare His righteousness and testify against an evil and perverse generation. God's faithful messengers beckon lost and misguided people to repentance. This marriage between Heaven and earth will release both God's kindness and severity.

The Holy Spirit resting in the hearts of His people will testify of His righteousness and bring conviction to the world concerning sin. The surest evidence of "children of Light" and God's true leadership is the clear presence of the Spirit's fruit—God's righteousness reflecting the Spirit's nature in our lives. The display of His character and the reflection of His Light are ultimately pleasing to the Lord. Allowing Christ to be fully formed in us will make us the "light" of the world possessing qualities consistent with "sons of the Kingdom" and children of light.

WALKING IN FRIENDSHIP

The Lord has identified those who occupy this unique position as His friends. What an incredible honor to be called God's friend; yet also a great responsibility that accompanies the commission for leadership. Jesus told His disciples:

> "No longer do I call you servants, for a servant does not
> know what his master is doing; but I have called you
> friends, for all things that I heard from My Father I have
> made known to you."
>
> —John 15:15, NKJV

The Lord's friends are capable of standing in this post with power and authority because of the refinement achieved in their lives. Intimate fellowship results from the testing of righteousness. It allows us to peer into God's heart to obtain understanding of His nature and character.

Scripture describes Daniel as one greatly beloved. This was true, at least in part, because of his heart for the nation and his willingness to stand in the gap for his people. He humbled himself in an attitude of repentance and foresight for the future. He presented supplications on behalf of those of his age, prior generations, and the generation of destiny that would see the restoration of God's temple.

Daniel's example is a prophetic foreshadowing of our role today. In this manner, divine purposes are birthed on earth through words anointed with Spirit and Life and expressed from a position of righteousness. Our Father chose the Body of Christ as Heaven's instrument to unfold His great redemptive plan. To fulfill our highest purpose, we too must discover that cherished and honorable position as the Lord's friends.

JUSTICE AND MERCY

Both justice and mercy are resident in the Father's heart. Justice calls for God's judgments to be established on earth; yet, His heart also yearns to release mercy when His representatives stand before Him as mediators between Heaven and earth. Like Moses, we remind Him of His loving-kindness and longsuffering nature.

Those with the unique distinction as His friends possess His divine nature and holy character and call attention to His great promises to each generation. The unveiling of mercy will stay His hand of judgment, giving a space of time for repentance.

It is always the enemy's desire to boast that the Lord was able to bring His people out of slavery, but not carry them into the promise. The Lord's friends continually petition the throne of grace with God's promises, and the expression of His divine attributes of loving-kindness and mercy.

God's friends will occupy this place of intercession on behalf of their generation, not because of their own merits, but because of His great compassion. From this position of favor we are allowed to intercede for others by calling upon His grace to grant hearts of repentance for the lost. This will lead them to the knowledge of the truth so they may escape the devil's snare, having been held captive by him to do his will.

> "If there is a messenger for him,
> A mediator, one among a thousand,
> To show man His uprightness,
> Then He is gracious to him, and says,
> 'Deliver him from going down to the Pit;
> I have found a ransom.'"
>
> —Job 33:23–24

Today we have a great opportunity to enter God's promises made to this generation and to those who have gone before us. A call to maturity is being heralded and God's grace is being extended to move us into divine destiny.

11

Signs of the Times

E vents of biblical proportion are occurring throughout the earth. Storms, earthquakes, celestial phenomena, death, political and natural upheaval, and personal losses all emphasize the mysterious nature of this present age. What does all this mean? That is a relevant question often asked of our ministry. We cannot afford to live in a state of blindness to the signs of the times.

During His earthly ministry, Jesus prophesied these conditions. He foretold that the spiritual and natural mood of Noah's generation would characterize our own. God's Word, and other historical documentation, confirms the wickedness, violence, and perversion permeating Noah's day. The Bible describes those times saying:

> God saw that the wickedness of man was great in the
> earth, and that every imagination of the thoughts of
> his heart was only evil continually...The earth also
> was corrupt before God, and the earth was filled with

> violence. And God looked upon the earth, and behold,
> it was corrupt; for all flesh had corrupted his way upon
> the earth.
>   —Genesis 6:5, 11–12, KJV

Certainly, a divine purpose and a biblical message are communicating themselves through these occurrences. A wondrous visitation of God's Spirit bearing great spiritual significance stands at the door, which, when fully released, will redefine modern perceptions of the Christian life, and influence society's every arena. Our wisest counsel is to properly interpret the prophetic signs and position ourselves to cooperate with God in His plan. Never before has there been greater need for God's grace and favor that is essential to launch us into this generation's destiny.

THE CAPSTONE GENERATION
No previous age has been given such profound promises yet been less capable of achieving them in our own strength. Recent years have clearly demonstrated this reality. J. Hudson Taylor emphasized:

> "Many Christians estimate difficulties in the light of
> their own resources, and thus attempt little and often
> fail in the little they attempt. All of God's giants have
> been weak men who did great things for God because
> they reckoned on His power and Presence with them."

Throughout the Western Church, pockets of anointing and favor have been discovered in some individuals and ministries. Even so, on the whole, the Church has been in a heightened season of refinement and grooming. In fact, many may consider it somewhat like the oppression and bondage experienced by God's people in the land of Egypt.

Regardless, God's mighty hand delivered His people from slavery with displays of grace and power eye had not seen nor ear heard! Such is our hope for this day as well: We need a never-before-seen demonstration of God's grace; however, we must contend for it if we are to watch the storehouses fill with the harvest.

The Bible declares that when the "capstone generation" emerges, it will be with shouts of "Grace, grace." Zechariah prophesied:

> This is the word of the LORD to Zerubbabel saying,
> "Not by might nor by power, but by My Spirit," says the
> LORD of hosts. What are you, O great mountain? Before
> Zerubbabel you will become a plain; and he will bring
> forth the top stone with shouts of "Grace, grace to it!"
> —Zechariah 4:6–7

In my battlefield vision, a great wave of divine favor overshadowed the end-of-the-age army providing God's anointing to overcome the enemy's final assault. It will be with shouts of "Grace, grace" that we joyfully articulate God's provision and intervention on behalf of His people.

SIGNS OF THE SEASON

Many signs are pointing to the great grace about to be released from God's throne to liberate and empower His people. Throughout our nation, numerous windstorms have caused extreme turmoil and devastation. Hurricanes Katrina and Ivan annihilated the coastal areas where we are based. Tornadoes sweep through many states with reckless abandon, resulting in considerable loss of life and property.

The windstorms rampaging throughout our nation are actually prophetic forecasts of approaching spiritual "winds of change." The natural winds are pointing to God's winds, which are the four spirits of heaven that stand before the Lord.

In a revelatory experience I was specifically given two Scriptures with prophetic application to our times. The Holy Spirit audibly highlighted the following two verses:

> The angel replied to me, "These are the four spirits of heaven, going forth after standing before the Lord of all the earth...
>
> —Zechariah 6:5

> ...and have tasted the good word of God and the powers of the age to come...
>
> —Hebrews 6:5

The Lord stressed that these two Scriptures are spiritually linked and identify what is eminently ahead. The four spirits of Heaven will facilitate the preparation of an overcoming body of saints who will "taste the good word of God and the powers of the Kingdom Age..." In modern Church history, only an isolated few have touched this realm in God, but those who did changed their generation.

Natural winds have been blowing to indicate that the four winds of the Spirit are poised for release. The Hebrew word *ruach* is translated "spirit" in Zechariah 6:5, meaning wind, or breath, of God.

> And the angel answered me, These are the four winds or spirits of the heavens, which go forth from presenting themselves before the Lord of all the earth. The chariot with the black horses is going forth into the north country, and the white ones are going forth after them [because there are two northern powers to overcome], and the dappled ones are going forth

toward the south country.

—Zechariah 6:5–6, AMP

Ezekiel describes four living creatures that surround God's throne. These are fascinating spiritual beings directly linked with the four winds prophesied through Zechariah. The language employed to describe each of the living creatures symbolically identifies God's attributes released to His people to empower them to overcome.

> Now as I looked at the living beings, behold, there was
> one wheel on the earth beside the living beings, for
> each of the four of them...Wherever the spirit was about
> to go, they would go in that direction. And the wheels
> rose close beside them; for the spirit of the living beings
> was in the wheels.

—Ezekiel 1:15, 20

God's prophet clearly recognized that the spirit or characteristics of the four living beings were manifested and revealed in the wheels. When the wheels of this mysterious spiritual visitation touched the earth, then the attributes resident in the four living beings were delegated to God's people.

When God visited Israel under the leadership of Moses, He had them orchestrate their camp in a specified way. They were instructed to surround the Tabernacle of Moses with three of Israel's tribes on each side. On each of the four sides a banner was assigned that highlighted the aspect of God's nature emphasized by the four living creatures surrounding His Throne.

East side: Judah represented by the face of a lion
South side: Reuben represented by the face of a man
West side: Ephraim represented by the face of an ox

North side: Dan represented by the face of an eagle

> When the cherubim stood still, the wheels would stand
> still; and when they rose up, the wheels would rise with
> them, for the spirit of the living beings was in them.
>
> —Ezekiel 10:17

The four living beings move in harmony and unison with the Holy Spirit. This phrase is reminiscent of Paul's words, "As many as are led by the Spirit of God, they are the sons of God." We are successful in God's Kingdom only to the extent that we yield ourselves to the Spirit's leadership and handiwork. He imparts the virtues we need to confront the spiritual opposition of our day. When the Ark of the Covenant touches the earth, representing a day of visitation, the attributes of the four living creatures will be imparted to God's people to empower them.

HEAVENLY ENDOWMENTS
The spiritual attributes represented by the lion, ox, man, and flying eagle are conveyed by God's winds or spirits to enable us overcome. The following is a brief synopsis of their applications:

FIRST LIVING CREATURE

> Then I saw when the Lamb broke one of the seven seals,
> and I heard one of the four living creatures saying as
> with a voice of thunder, "Come." I looked, and behold,
> a white horse, and he who sat on it had a bow; and a
> crown was given to him, and he went out conquering
> and to conquer.
>
> —Revelation 6:1–2

 1. **The lion**—an emblem of victory, authority, and

supremacy; symbol of kingship, royalty, and courage; the empowerment from God exemplified during the early apostolic age to gain great spiritual victories and sow the seeds of God's Kingdom on earth.

Following the Day of Pentecost, two spirits were introduced that would run concurrently throughout Church history. The first living creature, exemplified by the victorious lion, empowered the early Church to overcome political and religious persecution to establish an apostolic foundation. The false anointing, characterized by the white horse rider, portrayed a religious spirit that Paul, Jude, and other early apostolic leaders confronted within the Church.

Paul was a predominant messenger to this age and did not waiver from declaring the whole counsel of God. He set a standard for walking with the Lord in harmony, power, and revelatory knowledge of God's Kingdom authority.

The Gadites, when they joined David's army at Ziklag, were reputed to be mighty men of valor who had been trained for battle and were prolific at handling both shield and spear. The Bible says, "They possessed faces that were like the faces of lions." This expression captures the warlike attributes of the lion that existed among David's mighty men, which was likewise imparted by the Holy Spirit as an overcoming virtue.

SECOND LIVING CREATURE

When He broke the second seal, I heard the second living creature saying, "Come." And another, a red horse, went out; and to him who sat on it, it was granted to take peace from the earth, and that men would slay one another; and a great sword was given to him.

—Revelation 6:3–4

2. **The ox**—an emblem of sacrifice; a beast of burden. This
    is the spiritual impartation that was prominent from
    approximately AD 303–1520, and identified God's grace
    provided to believers who were martyred. It reached
    its pinnacle during the Dark Ages. The spirit of the ox
    empowered God's people to give themselves sacrificially.
    History records multiplied millions who were martyred
    during this age. It is written that many of these saints met
    their demise while singing hymns and rejoicing. They
    were imbued with a supernatural grace that enabled them
    to meet their destiny.

The ox was the spirit of the living creature granted to counter
the red horse that took peace from the earth and began the age
of martyrdom in the Smyrnan Church Age. The Smyrnan Age
overlaps with the continuation of the spirit of the lion and the
introduction of the spirit of the ox. All four spirits are present
on the earth during the Church ages; however, one is more
predominant during each of the horse riders.

The ox anointing, representing grace for sacrifice, counters
the red horse rider, representing persecution. The "ten days" of
persecution John mentions in Revelation 2:10 are generally taken
to include the final ten years of the most horrible persecution
of Diocletian, from AD 303–313. Nonetheless, he was the tenth
emperor to make such persecution a policy of government—ten
Roman emperors persecuted Christians as a matter of public
policy. Some historians perceive these emperors as ten "days" or
times of persecution and tribulation for this Church age. They are
as follows:

1. Nero (64 AD)   6. Severus (202)
2. Domitian (95)   7. Maximus (235)
3. Trajan (107)   8. Decius (249)

4. Hadrian (127)   9. Valerianus (257)
5. Aurelius (165)   10. Diocletian (303)

THIRD LIVING CREATURE

When He broke the third seal, I heard the third living
creature saying, "Come." I looked, and behold, a black
horse; and he who sat on it had a pair of scales in his
hand. And I heard something like a voice in the center
of the four living creatures saying, "A quart of wheat for
a denarius, and three quarts of barley for a denarius;
and do not damage the oil and the wine."

—Revelation 6:5–6

3. **The man**—this is the spirit of the reformers. Men and
    women were anointed with incredible wisdom and
    natural knowledge to reestablish the foundations of
    the faith lost during the Dark Ages. The spirit of the
    man provided the virtue to overcome the black horse
    rider, representing false teachings, dogmas, and human
    traditions. Christians were denied access to the Bible
    for many centuries. Although Wycliffe was the first to
    recognize the need to put God's Word into the people's
    hands, Martin Luther was the one who translated the
    Bible into common language and mass-produced it
    through the Gutenberg printing press. Many others
    followed in the Great Reformation leading up to the
    twentieth century.

This attribute of the Holy Spirit's anointing covered two Church
Ages—Sardis and Philadelphia—and extended from roughly
1512–1906. Men of great intellect and theological skill reaffirmed
the basic doctrines of the faith but also brought forward human

reasoning from the prior age mixed with it.

The Reformation Church had a revelation of justification by faith alone, apart from submitting to a priesthood of men, and that one need not belong to an earthly organization called "the church" in order to be part of the Church in God's eyes. This was the allotment of manna for their day and constituted progress but it was as far as they went. Their revelation was primarily concerning the feast of Passover and its prophetic meaning.

The sanctification message came in the day of John Wesley and George Whitefield. Their age continued the progressive revelation of Christ in the restoration process, but they had little or no revelation of either Pentecost or Tabernacles. While they received the gospel of justification/sanctification by faith alone, they were incapable of recognizing the spiritual impartations implied through Pentecost or embracing Sonship.

FOURTH LIVING CREATURE

> When the Lamb broke the fourth seal, I heard the voice
> of the fourth living creature saying, "Come." I looked,
> and behold, an ashen horse; and he who sat on it had
> the name Death; and Hades was following with him.
> Authority was given to them over a fourth of the earth,
> to kill with sword and with famine and with pestilence
> and by the wild beasts of the earth.
> —Revelation 6:7–8

4. **The flying eagle**—this is the spirit predominantly
    released in the present age epitomized in Ephesians
    1:17–18. The Spirit of Wisdom and Revelation is granting
    God's people access to the treasures of wisdom and
    knowledge hidden in Christ. It is the unfolding of the
    mysteries of God's Kingdom manifested in a body of

overcoming Christians. And it is His grace to live in
Heaven's revelatory realm.

The antichrist spirit has matured to a degree allowing it
to produce spiritual and natural death. Jesus prophesied this
confrontation in Matthew 13 with the illustration of the wheat
and tares. He taught that both Christ and antichrist spirits would
come to maturity at the harvest, symbolically portraying the end
of the age, which is happening now.

The antichrist spirit culminates in spiritual and natural death,
while God's Spirit is awakening His people to Heaven's reality
and the realization of manifesting His Kingdom on earth. We will
only taste an intimation of it on this side before the Lord returns,
but that introduction will transform the world and provoke the
great harvest.

The revelatory endowments represented by the flying eagle will
allow us to soar in the spirit and access divine mysteries preserved
for this generation. God's mystery will be made complete in this
generation, and that mystery is the revelation of Jesus Christ.
Jehovah of the Old Testament is Jesus of the New Testament!
In Him are the redemptive attributes of the Father expressed in
human form.

CULTIVATE HUMILITY

The humble will be delegated wonderful virtues from the
four living creatures, particularly that of the flying eagle,
exemplifying spiritual revelation. The last few years of Church
history, especially since the dramatic events of September 11,
2001, have been intended to cultivate humility in a body of
people to render them beneficiaries of exceedingly great grace.

Spiritually speaking, great grace surpasses common
grace; God has promised to give this favor to the humble
(1 Peter 5:5). This generation's spiritual and social needs

are prompting the most prodigious demonstration of God's grace ever bestowed on His people, for these shall be His champions entrusted with notable mantles of revelation and power essential for the harvest.

As Isaiah recorded, the Lord is looking for the humble and contrite:

> Thus says the LORD,
> "Heaven is My throne and the earth is My footstool.
> Where then is a house you could build for me?
> And where is a place that I may rest?
> For My hand made all these things,
> Thus all these things came into being," declares the
>   LORD.
> "But to this one I will look,
> To him who is humble and contrite of spirit,
> And who trembles at My word."
> —Isaiah 66:1–2

The ones who are lowly and tremble at God's Word will begin to experience divine intervention from the heavenly host uniquely prepared for this specific hour in human history. This scenario will facilitate the literal fulfillment of Hebrews 1:7—God's ministers will be ignited like flames of fire fanned by angels who are winds. Our grace is for the complete redemption of our soul—mind, will, and emotions—which will provide a platform for trustworthy stewards to be endowed with resurrection power. This will mark the introduction or tasting of the powers of the age to come.

Only from a place of submission can we carry God's tremendous virtue needed for the harvest of the ages. Kathryn Kuhlman was a twentieth century forerunner who discovered this place in God. In conferences and conventions, she publicly reiterated the beautiful experience of being filled with the Holy Spirit and apprehending

His gifts. Then she would venture deeper and ask, "But do you know the experience of having yielded your will to the will of the Father?" She identified the "secret place" in God and how it is accessed—through complete surrender. That is the ultimate example of spiritual humility.

To abandon our soul before God simply means to denounce, forsake, surrender, and relinquish our own thoughts and will to the Father. His thoughts and ways are much higher than our own. That does not mean that we eliminate our mind, but rather allow it to be transformed and renewed by the Spirit. Faithful believers, who press in to this place in Him, will be granted great grace to experience Heaven's winds.

THE WINDOWS OF HEAVEN

The windows of Heaven are being opened during this next season through which God's winds will blow. They will be the winds of:

1. Grace
2. Mercy
3. Deliverance
4. Wisdom

NORTH WIND — GRACE

The North wind of grace will open spiritual windows and doors granting access to the spiritual provision imperative in the harvest. Only God's grace and favor will make us the beneficiaries of our spiritual inheritance and participants in God's end-time plan!

Paul was set apart in his mother's womb for a specific calling on his life; nevertheless he stressed it was God's grace that transformed his way of life and launched his great apostolic ministry. His duty was to initiate the revelation of God's Kingdom mysteries. Our responsibility is to continue that model in the same fashion as Paul—an eventuality possible only by the revelation of

Jesus Christ (Galatians 1:12).

The treasures of wisdom and knowledge hidden in Christ are poised for release in this age. Apostolic leaders in the order of Paul, who emulate his intimate walk with Christ, will emerge with power and revelatory clarity through the winds of grace.

EAST WIND — MERCY

The East wind unleashes God's mercy. This results in the release of the Lord's compassion to cleanse and sanctify His people from the filth and corruption of this world. This wind will provide mercy to deliver us from our defilement. The revelation and application of the written Word imparts His spiritual DNA to rescue us from our carnal DNA (1 Corinthians 15:42–49). We are to bear the image of our heavenly Adam.

God's long suffering and indulgence with us is generally understood to be acts of kindness or compassion born of love and directly related to the state or condition of the ones to whom mercy is granted. The state of the ones receiving mercy is typically depicted as one of suffering and great need. We are a needy people; God's merciful grace is our only antidote.

According to Matthew 5, mercy is also granted to those who have sown forgiveness. A divine economy and exchange transpires producing amplified dividends when we are willing to comply with His standards.

> "FOR I WILL BE MERCIFUL TO THEIR INIQUITIES,
> AND I WILL REMEMBER THEIR SINS NO MORE."
> When He said, "A new covenant," He has made the
> first obsolete. But whatever is becoming obsolete and
> growing old is ready to disappear.
> —Hebrews 8:12–13

What an incredible demonstration of mercy, to be pardoned

and cleansed of unrighteous acts and the compulsive nature to continue in them! This truth demonstrates the superiority of the new covenant sealed with the Lord's blood. God's extraordinary mercy positions us with amazing opportunities to display in our generation the revelation of His Kingdom. Our iniquity is not only pardoned but erased, remembered no more. That is good news!

SOUTH WIND — DELIVERANCE
The South wind is the release of deliverance. This deposit of His grace will set free those held in prison and captivity by this world's oppressions and snares. The enemy has imprisoned the Body of Christ, but now the Lord has determined to bring deliverance. Many are captured by fear, lust, jealousy, anger, and no doubt many other tormenting adversaries. The Lord promised He would, "blow the trumpet, and will march in the storm winds of the south" (Zechariah 9:14).

The unveiling of this wind will bring liberty and freedom to those willing to abandon their souls and yield their wills to the Father's will:

> "THE SPIRIT OF THE LORD IS UPON ME, BECAUSE
> HE ANOINTED ME TO PREACH THE GOSPEL TO THE
>   POOR.
> HE HAS SENT ME TO PROCLAIM RELEASE TO THE
> CAPTIVES, AND RECOVERY OF SIGHT TO THE
>   BLIND,
> TO SET FREE THOSE WHO ARE OPPRESSED,
> TO PROCLAIM THE FAVORABLE YEAR OF THE
>   LORD."
>   —Luke 4:18–19

The South wind is the spirit of deliverance generated to mark a people prepared to inherit God's end-time promises. Throughout

Scripture, the term deliverance is most often associated with the concept of "drawing out" and "setting apart." It also entails rescue, recovery, and the possibility of escape for God's people from the enemy's oppression and embracing the freedom to worship God in Spirit and Truth.

Once delivered from the "net of the fowler," we are free to soar in the Heavens to receive additional wisdom and revelation essential for our maturity and growth. Deliverance can also be associated with childbirth; giving new life to something that has been germinating in the spiritual womb of the Body of Christ and thereby unveiling Kingdom purposes on earth.

WEST WIND—WISDOM

The west wind freely unharnessed symbolizes the revelatory anointing to unveil God's heavenly wisdom. It represents supernatural counsel to release His plans, purposes, and strategy to accomplish His mandates for this exceptional time in human history.

God's Word stresses every believer's right to be anointed with the Spirit of Wisdom and Revelation. This form of wisdom is not merely the ability to mentally analyze a situation and respond accordingly. This spiritual endowment allows a believer to venture deep into God's heart in order to perceive and understand His nature and the fullness of our redemptive rights.

Not only do we have the liberty to understand these mysteries, but the accompanying Spirit of Revelation offering illumination and comprehension of their reality. Paul recorded:

> ...that the God of our Lord Jesus Christ, the Father
> of glory, may give to you a spirit of wisdom and of
> revelation in the knowledge of Him. I pray that the
> eyes of your heart may be enlightened, so that you
> will know what is the hope of His calling, what are the

riches of the glory of His inheritance in the saints, and
what is the surpassing greatness of His power toward
us who believe. These are in accordance with the
working of the strength of His might...
                                        —Ephesians 1:17–19

The Spirit of Wisdom is more clearly defined as a supernatural
impartation of the Holy Spirit affording the ability to see
and recognize the Lord Jesus with a spiritual knowledge and
comprehension of His mysteries, plans, and purposes. Such a
heritage will reveal God's manifold and unsearchable secrets
hidden in Christ and additionally suggests deeper intimacy and
awareness of divine matters and intimates personal encounters
with the Lord.

The accompanying Spirit of Revelation grants a comprehension
of God's mysteries and attributes. It involves an understanding
and perception with our soul of things revealed in the Spirit. This
wisdom allows us not only to know the things of God, but also
the practical application of them on earth and in our lives.

The apostle Paul flourished in the operation of this gift.
This same endowment is essential in this generation to know
the concealed secrets reserved for the last days and share in
the hidden manna set aside for the end-time perfecting of the
Bride (Daniel 12:4).

When we read the words of Daniel's prophecy, our intellectual
minds detect the magnitude of their unfathomable promises. Even
so, when anointed with the Spirit of Wisdom and Revelation,
we obtain an experiential comprehension of them. The words
of the promises become living truth offered expression through
consecrated vessels. As 1 Corinthians 2:9, NKJV attests:

"Eye has not seen, nor ear heard,
Nor have entered into the heart of man

The things which God has prepared for those who love
Him."

The Spirit of Wisdom and Understanding provides the
articulation and comprehension of His "glorious inheritance
in the saints." This is the process of translating God's thoughts
into spiritual language.

Jeremiah 33:3's promise is a "now" word. As we call upon
God, the Spirit of Wisdom and Revelation releases insight
previously unknown. Having this insight demands a tremendous
responsibility of displaying godly character. The revelatory light
of this promise is so bright that it will necessitate God's great
grace to appropriate these truths and remain in that place with
longevity. Few people presently possess the purity of character
needed to access this wind in its fullness. Nevertheless, the
Bible predicts and promises that:

"Those who have insight will shine brightly like
the brightness of the expanse of heaven, and those
who lead the many to righteousness, like the stars
forever and ever. But as for you, Daniel, conceal
these words and seal up the book until the end of
time; many will go back and forth, and knowledge
will increase."
—Daniel 12:3–4

The Lord is promising, through His divine grace, to prepare
a body of people who will inherit these promises and begin to
access the supernatural provisions the spiritual winds illustrate.
Revelation 4:1 admonishes us to heed His voice as He beckons us
to come up higher through the door standing open in Heaven,
and receive access to Him and the unveiling of His Kingdom.

ACCESS TO THE HEAVENLY ARMORY

Bob Jones is one of my wife's and my close friends and moves with a clear prophetic anointing. He was given a vision from the Lord that emphasizes the truth I am sharing. His revelation highlighted God's armory being opened with an escalation in the release of spiritual provision for this notable hour.

The storehouse Bob was shown contained weapons of our warfare and spiritual endowments supplied to God's army for the confrontations ahead. It was apparent in the revelation that immediate access to this armory was mandatory. He was given the Scripture:

> The LORD has opened His armory
> And has brought forth the weapons of His indignation,
> For it is a work of the Lord GOD of hosts
> In the land of the Chaldeans.
> —Jeremiah 50:25

We are presently being called to enter into our priestly ministry of Revelation 3:20. Our response to this call will determine whether we are allowed to proceed into the overcoming role mentioned in Revelation 3:21. Those who experience the Lord in this manner, and share in His victory, endowed with the virtue of overcomers, will hear the invitation to "come up here" through the open door of Revelation 4:1.

> "Behold, I stand at the door and knock. If anyone hears
> My voice and opens the door, I will come in to him and
> dine with him, and he with Me. To him who overcomes
> I will grant to sit with Me on My Throne, as I also
> overcame and sat down with My Father on His Throne."
> —Revelation 3:20–21, NKJV

After these things I looked, and behold, a door standing
open in heaven. And the first voice which I heard was
like a trumpet speaking with me, saying, "Come up
here, and I will show you things which must take place
after this."

—Revelation 4:1, NKJV

From this heavenly perspective, much will be revealed and
accessed. Spiritual provisions of vital importance to fulfill our
divine mandate for the harvest are in heavenly places containing
the saints' inheritance. The apostle Paul articulated this reality
in Ephesians 1:3 when he stated, "Blessed be the God and Father
of our Lord Jesus Christ, who has blessed us with every spiritual
blessing in the heavenly places in Christ."

Heaven's armory, to which we now have more extensive
access, is a prophetic portrayal of the divinely powerful weapons
provided for us through Christ's sufferings, and more importantly
His resurrection. This arsenal is our inheritance in Him, and to
apprehend it, we must gain entrance to the heavenly places where
He is seated.

God desires to delegate resurrection life. In this spiritual
armory are mantles of authority and power as well as great
ministries of healing and creative miracles that will result in
restored limbs and organs. Our calling is to take a fortified
stand and determine to carry prominent spiritual endowments
as trustworthy stewards. When the apostolic leaders of the early
Church encountered God in their upper room experience, they
emerged aggressively in an offensive posture that displaced
God's ancient enemies in strategic regions.

In Bob's revelatory experience, when God's people made the
decision to stand, they saw themselves confronted with a powerful
spirit of divination that had been releasing much confusion
and false prophetic proclamations in and through the Church.

Surprisingly, with the fortitude that now emanated from this army, the victory was swift and sure in the battles assigned to us by the Holy Spirit.

Once God's army took their stand, they didn't even need to advance. It was as if they were standing in the gap and the enemy had to pass through them to get to believers. Fortunately, because of the spiritually provided weapons, the enemy was unsuccessful in proceeding around, over, or through those called and anointed for leadership. God's plan for His government on earth is to confront the spiritual influences plaguing the Body of Christ. Then we will be more capable of reaching our generation with a harvest of souls. The victory must be achieved among God's people first.

DEFENDING OUR LENTIL FIELDS

The Lord is a warrior and those who share in His warlike attributes will no longer run from the enemy or subsist in a defensive mode. They have chosen to take a stand! One of David's mighty men was Shammah, a Haraite, or "mountain dweller." With boldness and courage he decided he would not run from the Philistines as others had done; instead he took his stand to defend a lentil field against overwhelming odds, and the Lord prevailed with him for a great victory. Many will dwell on the Lord's mountain to be favored with the valor and heroism of Shammah. 2 Samuel 23:11–12 records:

> Now after him was Shammah the son of Agee a
> Hararite. And the Philistines were gathered into a troop
> where there was a plot of ground full of lentils, and the
> people fled from the Philistines. But he took his stand
> in the midst of the plot, defended it and struck the
> Philistines; and the LORD brought about a great victory.

For many years the Church has been in a progressive restoration of her biblical and apostolic heritage. That reestablishment process began with the reformers and has escalated over the last century in the careful and meticulous unfolding of God's heavenly blueprint. Through numerous expressions of spiritual outpouring, great and valuable truth has been recovered to the Church as her legacy in Christ. As in the days of David's mighty man, the spirit of the Philistines has attempted to steal or destroy the "lentil fields" of truth planted by past spiritual pioneers.

Part of the strategy of the enemy in this ploy has been to undermine, destroy, or discredit past messengers in order to corrupt the message. But the Spirit of Truth will prevail and attain maturity and fruitfulness in this generation. Notice that an unknown farmer planted the field, but Shammah defended the lentils with strength and great courage.

NO LONGER IN CAVES
For a season David and his militant band hid in caves from the oppression of Saul. The Bible records that:

> David departed from there and escaped to the cave of
> Adullam; and when his brothers and all his father's
> household heard of it, they went down there to him.
> —1 Samuel 22:1

This was temporarily necessary for survival, however, it was only for a season. When the appropriate time arrived, David emerged as an awesome leader and warrior to overcome Israel's enemies. The time of hiding in the caves has come to an end!

God's armory is now accessible through the open-door invitation presently set before us. The time has arrived! Spiritual confrontations with our adversary will substantially escalate, and the realization that the Lord has made provision for our victory is of great comfort. Joel prophesied this battle saying:

Proclaim this among the nations:
Prepare a war; rouse the mighty men!
Let all the soldiers draw near, let them come up!
Beat your plowshares into swords
And your pruning hooks into spears;
Let the weak say, "I am a mighty man."
—Joel 3:9–10

The armory depicted in Jeremiah 50:25 has dual qualities of both military armament and natural provision. It serves as a treasury or storehouse, used for the storage of royal treasure and weaponry. A number of mature Christians received the divine promise of seeing the "warehouse of God" manifested on the earth before their deaths. That day is imminent! The contents of God's Heavenly storehouse containing our spiritual inheritance are about to be fully introduced.

THE WEAPON OF CHOICE

An interesting aspect of Bob's vision is that He watched the Lord specifically choose the battle-axe from the spiritual arsenal to be the weapon of choice for the approaching confrontation. These axes will be laid to the root of the Babylonian tree of confusion. In the vision, it was as if the Church had been in a defensive posture. Now is the time to transition into turning and facing our enemy with more readily available heavenly provision.

We were armed for battle in the armory of God. There are multiple layers of meaning to the choice of weapons initiated by the Lord. The battle-axe has a very specific use that highlights our commissioning to deal with precepts of man, confusion, counterfeit revelation, and false teachings that have kept the Church from her high calling. The prophet David once declared:

Draw also the spear and the battle-axe to meet those

who pursue me;
Say to my soul, "I am your salvation."

—Psalm 35:3

The prince of Persia was able to withstand and hinder the heavenly provision sent to Daniel. However, he was only able to do so for a limited season. Prayers, intercession, and prophetic proclamations in agreement with Heaven will weaken demonic shields and uncover works of darkness.

In Bob's vision, a holy determination was imparted to the Church for this season. A stalwart spirit prevailed in the people who overcame fear and timidity which loosed an unyielding spiritual boldness. This was not because of any strength of ours, but because of the Victorious One standing with us.

The spirit of Babylon has attempted to imprison the Body of Christ in a dungeon of confusion, self-promotion, humanistic agendas, and unbelief. A day of liberation has come, but it will be a battle. In the vision, Bob specifically noted that the warriors had a battle-axe in each hand. No shield was provided. The Lord emphasized that we will be one another's shield.

This war will require unity and fraternal affection so we can cover one another's backs in an all-out offensive maneuver. Our defensive implement is one another and God's Spirit resident in our co-laborers. We are the Lord's provision and shield for the ones to whom we are joined through the spirit of agreement. Furthermore, in the vision, the warriors wielded the battle-axes with such expertise and precision, that it was difficult for the adversary to release his weapons against this army. The confrontation was violent, but the victory was sure.

CHAPTER

12

The Master
of Breakthrough

Τhe angel stated his name is Breakthrough and he has
been assigned to the United States. This was articulated
to Bob Jones in one of the most significant visitations he
has ever received.

For many years I have watched the revelatory realm open to
Bob in profound ways. I was astounded that he recently had the
second-most powerful visitation of his life. The only one higher
engendered directly from the Lord Jesus Himself.

On Friday, March 24, 2006, as Bob was preparing for
prayer, he immediately fell into an Acts 10:10 type of trance.
Bob's highest revelations come in this way. As the visitation
commenced, Bob saw what appeared to be twelve ordinary
"men" approaching him. Although they had the appearance of
men, he knew they were angels. The one in front seemed to be
the most prominent and served as spokesman for the group.

He said, "My name is Breakthrough, and I have now been
assigned to the United States." For approximately thirty minutes
the angel shared with Bob historical accounts of past revivals

that had transpired to God's glory and the angel's involvement in them. His job is to release breakthrough and awakening, initiating a wave of harvest by extracting all obstacles to God's plans while the other angels gather the harvest.

Most prominently, Breakthrough shared about his intimate involvement in the life of Benson Idahosa, a powerful man of God in ministry throughout Nigeria and other African nations. The angel specifically explained that he had once been assigned to Nigeria but had been reassigned to America.

The angel told Bob of influential revivals he was responsible for that had brought many souls into God's Kingdom. Bob had had no foreknowledge of these historical events. Breakthrough informed Bob that he had been in the United States for approximately two years laying the groundwork for the next revival. A revival, he avowed, that present stadiums are not adequate to hold once it is fully manifested.

This revelation was particularly significant for me, as it directly related to my experience of seeing the "angels that gather" in October, 2003. "Angels that gather" will not only collect the wheat into the barn but will also extract stumbling blocks that interfere with the flourishing of God's Kingdom—the spiritual provision Bob was seeing in his experience highlighted how the main angel provided breakthrough while the others gathered the harvest.

BOB'S VISION CONTINUED

The angel called Breakthrough continued to inform Bob about God's end-time strategy. He shared how Benson Idahosa was often commissioned into a nation or region with God's mandate. No matter what the opposition was, all obstacles were removed through Breakthrough so a harvest of souls could be achieved. That is the model for these coming days and our promised harvest.

The angel next told Bob that everything he was observing in this vision was a prophecy. He asked, "What do you see?"

Bob replied that the appearance of the twelve angels seemed so ordinary. The angel responded, "Precisely—we are going to work with ordinary people who have fully yielded their spirit, soul, and body to the Lord."

Those used most prominently in this installment of God's plan will not boast in their wisdom or might, but in knowing the Lord intimately. Jeremiah 9:23–24 bespeaks this attribute:

> ..."Let not a wise man boast of his wisdom, and let not the mighty man boast of his might, let not a rich man boast of his riches; but let him who boasts boast of this, that he understands and knows Me, that I am the Lord who exercises lovingkindness, justice and righteousness on earth; for I delight in these things," declares the Lord.

The Lord intends during this season to fully mobilize the Body of Christ into its function as God's intermediary on earth. Fivefold ministry's foremost responsibility is to equip God's people to do the work of the ministry. Even the feeblest among us should be as noble and victorious as the formidable worshiping-warrior, King David (Zechariah 12:8).

MOVE, MOVE, MOVE

Breakthrough shouted, "Move, move, move!" From this Bob recognized there would be at least three major expressions of this spiritual dynamic soon to take place. The shouted command also articulated our directive to move in faith on earth in order to cooperate in the spirit with this heavenly host. This is an end-time strategy we should employ now.

The predominant Scripture directing us in this commissioning is Matthew 10:7–8 declaring:

And as you go, preach, saying, "The kingdom of heaven
is at hand.' Heal the sick, raise the dead, cleanse the
lepers, cast out demons. Freely you received, freely give.

We are approaching a season of harvest—of souls and promises.
Even so, its advent will not be through the mere articulation of
words but accompanied by demonstrations of power. The early
Church adhered to this pattern, as did the life and ministry of
Benson Idahosa.

In Exodus 23, God promised to send an Angel before Israel
to overcome every enemy and establish them in the land of
promise. Their obedience to the Word assured their victory and
released the Lord to remove sickness from their midst. In like
fashion, a wave of healing will accompany the season of grace
we are now entering.

KNOWING THE TIMING

Every leader we are in relationship with recognizes the need for
breakthrough in the Western Church, and our written and spoken
messages are built around this reality. Traveling the nation, I
have encountered an epidemic of hopelessness I know the Lord
intends to reverse. Spiritual vision from the revelatory realm
of Heaven provides hope derived by a revelation of our calling
and destiny; hope dispels hopelessness. Such is the promise of
Ephesians 1:17–18.

It is not difficult to discern our present condition. Nevertheless,
I personally desire to be a loyal servant like the ones who ventured
into the Promised Land and returned with a faith and hope filled
report as in Moses' day. Yes, there are giants in the land, but God is
abundantly able to empower us to overcome. This impartation will
strengthen our feeble knees and encourage our downcast hearts.

The prophet Ezekiel was transported to a valley of dry
bones. He was not instructed to condemn them but to prophesy

life to them. He related:

> So I prophesied as He commanded me, and the breath
> came into them, and they came to life and stood on
> their feet, an exceedingly great army. Then He said to
> me, "Son of man, these bones are the whole house of
> Israel; behold, they say, 'Our bones are dried up and our
> hope has perished. We are completely cut off.' Therefore
> prophesy and say to them, 'Thus says the Lord GOD,
> "Behold, I will open your graves and cause you to come
> up out of your graves, My people; and I will bring you
> into the land of Israel.'"
>
> —Ezekiel 37:10–12

That is our hope and expectation. We desire to breathe life into dry bones and watch them animate with life forming a force of overcomers.

Though the Western Church may resemble a valley of dry bones, I believe the Lord views her prophetically as an exceedingly formidable army. We are convinced our nation has an incredible destiny still to be fulfilled. When people are given a glimpse of their individual role in that destiny, they are transformed and propelled on course toward repentance and the impartation of the Christ-like nature.

They realize God's cause and are forever changed, and the joy of their salvation is restored. We notice that happening now. Strongholds of hopelessness, despair, depression, and other oppressive mind-sets will be overcome when God's "zoe" life is breathed into His army.

LORD OF THE BREAKTHROUGH

The presence of the angels will resemble the spiritual sign given to King David in his battle with the Philistines in 2 Samuel 5.

When David inquired of the Lord for divine strategy and precise timing, the Lord released breakthrough to rout all opposition and win a complete victory! The Scripture relates:

> So David came to Baal-perazim, and defeated them there; and he said, "The LORD has broken through my enemies before me like the breakthrough of waters." Therefore he named that place Baal-perazim [the master of breakthrough].
> —2 Samuel 5:20

Victory is achieved in the spirit realm first then manifested in the natural realm. In the continuation of this prophetic scenario, the Bible recounts that David knew to move against his enemies when he discerned the wind blowing among the balsam trees.

Following that example, we will learn in this day to cooperate with the Lord's timing when we discern God's winds, manifested through His angels, moving on our behalf. Heaven and earth will cooperate in this powerful dynamic (Hebrews 1:7).

Finally, when the angel again questioned Bob about what he saw, the only other dynamic in the vision Bob could perceive was the angel's friendly demeanor. That in itself is also a prophecy. The end-time Church will learn to cooperate fully with the spiritual host assigned to us in the same way friends learn to work cohesively in unison with their closest friends.

It is our responsibility to meticulously follow the Holy Spirit's leadership so every spiritual dynamic and resource allotted to us may be fully activated. We release on the earth what we discern in the spirit.

JUDAH'S TWINS

One final Scripture reference the angel gave Bob in his visitation came from Genesis 38:27–30. In this passage we discover the birthing of Judah's twins. The messenger emphasized the prophetic significance of the names given to these infants as a parabolic picture.

Perez—Breach
Zarach—Dawning or rising

If we are to qualify to be utilized in this spiritual move we must possess both boldness and determination. It would be a grave breach for us to put our hand to this task and then withdraw it. According to Hebrews 10:37–39, NKJV "For yet a little while, and He who is coming will come and will not tarry. Now the just shall live by faith; But if anyone draws back, My soul has no pleasure in him."

But we are not of those who draw back to perdition, but of those who believe to the saving of the soul. We cannot be among those who retreat on account of opposition or fear; rather, among those who press forward to witness breakthrough achieved.

A CONFIRMING VISITATION

As an additional confirmation to Bob Jones' revelation, the Lord also graced a friend of ours with a visit while in Nigeria in 2004, conferring the same revelation. At the same time I authored an article outlining the vision of the "angels that gather," our friend, Pastor Randy Demain, had accepted an invitation to participate on a missionary trip to Nigeria.

While in an open-air meeting, Randy watched as the Holy Spirit accomplished virtually every manifestation we read about in the book of Acts. Mighty miracles, signs, and wonders punctuated this meeting, and numerous souls entered God's Kingdom through that demonstration of His Spirit.

That evening when Randy returned to his room he was so excited he could not sleep and decided simply to worship the

Lord. As he did, he heard an audible voice ask, "I have a gift for you; and will you receive it?"

Much to his surprise the Lord was asking if he would be willing to accept a spiritual gift. When he responded affirmatively, Randy perceived with his open eyes an angel the Lord desired to assign him. His name was Breakthrough Revival.

The Lord next explained to Randy that this angel had been assigned to Benson Idahosa until his death in 1998. The Lord shared how Breakthrough removes all obstacles and stumbling blocks so God's people can entreat the Lord of the Harvest and reap a bountiful gathering of souls. Both Randy and Bob encountered the same angel.

Later Randy returned home and read our newsletter outlining this exact end-time strategy confirming what had been explained in his visitation. Since 2004, Randy and I have since been sharing this revelation, laying the groundwork for a wave of harvest. We believe this will initially be a harvest of harvesters.

HARVESTERS ARISE

One final confirmation concerning this generation's promised harvest arrived only days before this book was scheduled to go to print. While in Dudley, England, to speak at a prophetic conference, I met Surprise Sithole, African director of Partners in Harvest. He helps oversee, with Rolland and Heidi Baker, over six thousand Churches birthed through Iris Ministries in Mozambique, Africa. Notable miracles the Lord performed through this man of God are on record. On my behalf the Lord used Surprise to offer the final affirmation that this is the season for a harvest of harvesters.

In my session, I began to speak about the revelation of the present mandate to entreat the Lord of the Harvest to gather laborers into the barn to be trained and mentored through a season of accelerated equipping for the great harvest. When I shared this revelation, Surprise grew very excited and mentioned that this was the first time a revelation given to him three years before had been confirmed.

He related to the group how in 2004, he had been in a service and found himself troubled by some of what had transpired. He immediately went to his hotel room and knelt on the floor to pray. When he did, he felt a sensation of ascending, similar to what one would experience in a very fast elevator.

When he opened his eyes, he realized he was having a heavenly experience. There before him stood the Ancient of Days with millions of people prostrate before Him in adoration and worship. The transition from the natural to the spiritual realm had shifted so suddenly he was uncertain what had transpired. The Ancient of Days assured him he was experiencing a divine revelation with a strategic purpose.

Surprise then found himself holding fruit. With this realization, he also saw Enoch and Elijah standing at a distance. His first inclination was to share this fruit with them. However, the Ancient of Days informed him that the fruit was not for them but for the people of the earth.

The Ancient of Days counseled, "Take this fruit and share it with your brethren in the earth, and tell the harvesters to arise." Surprise was overwhelmed by that statement's magnitude. "How?" he asked. The Lord answered, "The gifts are coming." Finally, Surprise asked one more question: "When?" With that final question the millions who had been prostrate before the Lord stood to their feet and simultaneously shouted, "NOW!"

I was thrilled beyond description to hear Surprise share this testimony of his heavenly experience. He heard directly from the Lord's lips the directive for the "harvesters to arise." This gave me the final confirmation of our entry into a season that will exhibit both the fruit of the Spirit and the power of God. The purpose of this impartation will be to gather a wave of harvest consisting primarily of harvesters to be used in the great harvest.

EMBRACING OUR OPPORTUNITY
We have reached a "fullness of time" juncture in Church history. God's end-time plan is being catapulted in motion with a "breakthrough" anointing. Naturally, this is not all He is doing but certainly it is a vital part.

> The LORD has opened His armory
> And has brought forth the weapons of His indignation;
> For it is a work of the Lord GOD of hosts
> In the land of the Chaldeans.
> —Jeremiah 50:25

Days of divine visitation and breakthrough are noticeably marked with the miraculous. The Latter Rain Revival initiated in 1946, is remembered as one of the most significant expressions of God's miracle working power recorded in modern Church history. Many historians consider it the greatest outpouring of power since the inception of the Church and view it as a prototype of the days ahead.

We are privileged in this generation to have numerous audio and video recordings of those meetings available. We are able to learn from the men and women who were the instruments of God's power, how to steward God's supernatural dimension.

TWENTY-SIX CREATIVE MIRACLES
Many notable miracles are on record, but one of the most significant accounts occurred in March, 1959, through the ministry of A. A. Allen. A small boy received twenty-six creative miracles in one service.

R. W. Schambach was A. A. Allen's worship leader at the time and shares his eyewitness account of this miracle and his role in it. He testifies how this young boy's mother sought him out on the last day of a week of healing meetings. She had traveled with her son from their home in Knoxville, Tennessee, to Birmingham pursuing supernatural healing for him. That was his only hope since the best of the medical field had given up on him and offered her no hope for his survival.

The four-year-old lad was born with twenty-six major diseases. He was blind in his right eye, deaf, and dumb, and his tongue protruded from his mouth and rested upon his chin. His arms and legs were deformed and totally useless—twisted against his body. He had no feet, was partially paralyzed, and remained curled in a fetal position since birth. He had no male organs, and every other major organ in his body suffered from numerous complications. Most doctors had not expected him to live until his first birthday. Despite that prognosis, he was now four years old and in desperate need of God's touch.

The young mother had been to every service for a week, this was the final day. At that time the ministers used prayer cards to determine who to pray for. Unfortunately, her prayer card was never called. She personally approached Brother Schambach and implored him to help get her son to the man of God for prayer. Brother Schambach promised he would, but that never became necessary, since the Lord had other plans.

When the service began, A. A. Allen took an offering that challenged the congregation to extend their faith into the supernatural realm. As a gesture of faith, this young mother was the first to put twenty dollars in the offering basket. Like the widow woman Jesus remarked about, this amount was all she had. As the man of God began the service, he stopped his preaching and announced he was going into a spiritual vision.

In his vision, Allen found himself in the maternity ward of a hospital where an infant had just been born. He saw the doctors pronounce a death sentence on the boy with twenty-six major illnesses. He then watched in his vision as the mother entered an old Ford automobile and drove to that very meeting. He then summoned the mother to bring the young boy up for prayer.

When he offered the prayer of faith, R. W. Schambach testifies that with his own eyes he saw God's power overshadow the boy. First the tongue of the little fellow corrected itself back inside his mouth. Next pools of light entered his eye sockets and beautiful brown eyes were supernaturally restored. He then watched his bones begin to snap and crack as his legs and arms came into their perfect place.

Then, Schambach watched as the two legs that had no feet suddenly began to change as feet were supernaturally created before the three-thousand in attendance. All of his internal organs were perfectly restored. Finally, his tongue was supernaturally allowed to speak his first words: "Mama."

I have personally spoken with individuals who witnessed this event firsthand, and medical doctors' affidavits were provided to A. A. Allen's ministry to verify the miracle. This is a token of the kind of creative miracles we are promised in this generation following breakthrough.

SIMPLICTY AND PURITY OF DEVOTION
Our role is to continue to pursue the simplicity and purity of devotion to Christ Jesus and become men and women of prayer. This empowers the spiritual host to battle in the spiritual realm on our behalf to achieve notable victories to the Lord's glory.

There is a spiritual principle that states where evil abounds, grace does much more abound. Undoubtedly, our nation is in trouble. Nevertheless, the Lord is extending an incredible opportunity for His great grace to institute breakthrough. We must embrace every divine opportunity and employ the incredible gifts being delegated to us at this crucial moment in human history. Breakthrough is at hand and a harvest of harvesters will be gathered.

About the Author

Paul Keith Davis and his wife Wanda founded WhiteDove Ministries after the Lord sovereignly sent a beautiful white dove to them as a prophetic sign of their calling. They have traveled extensively speaking at conferences and churches imparting the end-time mandate of preparation for the Glory and Manifest Presence of Christ.

Paul Keith has written three books—*The Thrones of Our Soul, Engaging the Revelatory Realm of Heaven,* and *Books of Destiny*—as well as a number of articles appearing in Christian publications, including *Charisma* magazine, the *MorningStar Journal,* and *Church Growth International.* For each of the past several years, he has also written with Bob Jones the prophetic book entitled *The Shepherd's Rod.* This booklet has been widely circulated in this country and abroad with an emphasis on providing insight with understanding concerning the mobilization of the Church for her high calling and glorious destiny.

He has spent many years in an extensive study highlighting the ministry of revelation and power exemplified throughout the Church Ages with an emphasis on the twentieth century Church. His heart's desire is to see the full restoration of biblical apostolic ministry manifested through the Spirit of Truth residing in God's people expressing salvation, healing, and deliverance to the Glory of God and His Christ.

Paul Keith and Wanda, reside in Orange Beach, Alabama. Together they have five children and four grandchildren.

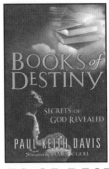
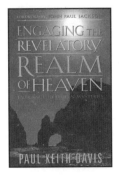